The media's watching Vault!
Here's a sampling of our coverage.

"For those hoping to climb the ladder of success, [Vault's] insights are priceless."
– *Money* magazine

"The best place on the web to prepare for a job search."
– *Fortune*

"[Vault guides] make for excellent starting points for job hunters and should be purchased by academic libraries for their career sections [and] university career centers."
– *Library Journal*

"The granddaddy of worker sites."
– *U.S. News and World Report*

"A killer app."
– *The New York Times*

One of Forbes' 33 "Favorite Sites."
– *Forbes*

"To get the unvarnished scoop, check out Vault."
– *Smart Money* Magazine

"Vault has a wealth of information about major employers and job-searching strategies as well as comments from workers about their experiences at specific companies."
– *The Washington Post*

"A key reference for those who want to know what it takes to get hired by a law firm and what to expect once they get there."
– *New York Law Journal*

"Vault [provides] the skinny on working conditions at all kinds of companies from current and former employees."
– *USA Today*

> the most trusted name in career information™

VAULT GUIDE TO
EDUCATION CAREERS

BY JENNIFER BAKER
and the staff of vault

Library of Congress CIP Data is available.

ISBN 13 : 978-1-58131-622-3

ISBN 10 : 1-58131-622-4

Printed in the United States of America

ACKNOWLEDGMENTS

Jennifer Baker's acknowledgments: Special thanks go to the professionals who contributed their time and wisdom to the creation of this book: Debbie Beaudin, Rosemary Baker, James De Francesco, Chad Hamilton, Samuel Jordan, Clara Lin, Betsy Sullivan, Brigid Tileston, Jim Tileston, Steve Tullin, and Rachel Wadle.

Vault's acknowledgments: We are extremely grateful to Vault's entire staff for all their help in the editorial, production and marketing processes. Vault also would like to acknowledge the support of our investors, clients, employees, family and friends. Thank you!

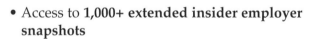
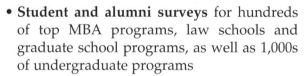

Table of Contents

Visit Vault at **www.vault.com** for insider company profiles, expert advice, career message boards, expert resume reviews, the Vault Job Board and more.

VAULT CAREER LIBRARY   vii

Visit Vault at **www.vault.com** for insider company profiles, expert advice,
career message boards, expert resume reviews, the Vault Job Board and more.

VAULT CAREER LIBRARY

ix

Visit Vault at **www.vault.com** for insider company profiles, expert advice,
career message boards, expert resume reviews, the Vault Job Board and more.

VAULT CAREER LIBRARY   xi

Visit Vault at www.vault.com for insider company profiles, expert advice,
career message boards, expert resume reviews, the Vault Job Board and more.

VAULT CAREER LIBRARY   xiii

Introduction

Nearly one in four Americans is an enrolled student at any given time. This enormous segment of the U.S. population encompasses people of all ages and from all walks of life. American students have a wide range of educational goals—from learning their ABCs to obtaining an MD—but each of these students needs the support of dedicated educators in order to obtain the knowledge and skills they need. As a result of this great demand for talented educators there are job opportunities for teachers in every geographical region of the country. Education is America's second largest industry, and the different career tracks within education are as varied as the national population of its students.

Despite the wide variety of jobs within education, the things that attract professionals to the field are often similar. The people who become educators usually have a sincere desire to make a difference in the lives of others—they remember the teachers who helped them to reach their own goals, and are thrilled by the possibility that they might be able to inspire others in the same way. The classroom can be a challenging place to work, but for the passionate teacher there is no greater joy than watching students grasp a challenging concept, or finding a way to capture students' imagination and spark their curiosity. Successful teachers are dedicated to achieving this goal, and often have a tenacious belief in the power of education to transform students' lives.

Not just teachers

However, the field of education is not limited to teachers. There are thousands of job opportunities for administrators, paraprofessionals, counselors, social workers, media specialists and other professionals in American schools, and these professionals are integral to the school environment. Like classroom teachers, these educators are committed to giving students the support they need in order to reach their full potential.

In recent years, the decisions of politicians have put a great deal of pressure on teachers and schools to perform—frequently in working conditions that are less than ideal. As a result, many educators often struggle not to maintain their enthusiasm and avoid becoming "burned out" as they struggle to improve student performance with meager resources. Many

Visit Vault at **www.vault.com** for insider company profiles, expert advice, career message boards, expert resume reviews, the Vault Job Board and more.

VAULT CAREER LIBRARY

1

people believe that teachers work short days, but the reality is that most teachers spend much of their free time planning lessons and grading papers.

A career in education can offer enormous challenges as well as enormous rewards. As a result, you may have doubts about whether or not education is the right field for you. The information in this book will help you determine this. And if you know that you want to become an educator but are unsure of the exact career path you want to take, this book will give you a clearer vision of the specific career in education that is right for you.

THE SCOOP

EDUCATION CAREERS

A Brief History of Education in the United States

CHAPTER 1

Early American Schools

The first public schools in America were formed during colonial times, when local laws mandating school attendance were established in areas throughout the American Northeast. Colonial schools placed a great deal of emphasis on religious studies, along with the traditional "three Rs" (reading, writing and arithmetic). In the South, there were few public schools during colonial times; wealthy southern families typically hired private tutors to educate their children.

The common school movement

Up until the 1800s, public schools were governed entirely by local authorities. The quality of education varied greatly from region to region, and in many areas of the country there were no public schools at all. As a result, in the early 19th century, a reform movement began, with the goal of standardizing education throughout the United States through government regulations. One of the reformers' primary goals was to organize state departments of education that would oversee the activities of local school districts. Another goal was to deemphasize the role of religious studies in public education, placing a greater emphasis on civic instruction, which they believed was key to helping the growing immigrant population become integrated into American life.

The reformists' activities, known as the Common School Movement, were controversial at the time. Industry leaders resisted the idea of mandatory school attendance because this would deprive them of child laborers. And Roman Catholics feared that the new public school systems would have a bias towards Protestant values. However, in the end, the Common School Movement was largely successful in changing the structure of public education in America.

Despite the widespread reforms, the Common School Movement extended only to K-8 education. Public high schools were relatively rare until well into the 20th century, existing only in large cities. Throughout the 20th century secondary, high school education became increasingly available. Now all 50 states have laws requiring children to attend school until the age of 16.

Brown vs. the Board of Education

Public schools in the United States were plagued by racial inequality from the beginning. Prior to the Civil War, African-Americans were rarely educated in a formal school setting. The Common School Movement's goal of making public education available to "all children" only extended to the education of all white children.

Eventually, public education was made available to children of all races, but in many parts of the United States, schools were segregated. The legality of this was established by a ruling in the late 1800s, which stated that government-funded facilities could be segregated by race, so long as they were "separate but equal." In 1951, a group of parents from Topeka, Kansas challenged this idea in the U.S. Supreme Court, where the case was considered to be representative of several similar legal battles taking place in southern cities. The plaintiffs argued that segregated schools, by their very nature, were unequal, and the Supreme Court agreed.

The process of desegregation lasted until well into the second part of the 20th century. In fact, many experts in the field of education believe that the fight for truly integrated schools offering continues into the present, because of the many low-performing schools that exist in low-income, minority communities throughout the country.

The No Child Left Behind Act

In 2001, Congress, led by President George W. Bush, passed a law regulating public education programs across the country. No Child Left Behind Act (or NCLB) was created with the purpose of setting equal expectations for all public schools in the United States, by holding them accountable for the performance of their students.

The specific mandates of NCLB cover a great deal of territory, from requiring schools to administer standardized tests at regular intervals to requiring that public schools give lists of student names and addresses to military recruiters. NCLB is a historic law, in that it is the first sweeping educational reform law ever to be passed by the federal government, taking much of the decision-making power away from state departments of education.

NCLB is controversial within the education community for several reasons. For one thing, although it imposes dozens of mandates on public schools, it does not allocate any federal funding towards the implementation of these mandates. As a result, many school districts have been forced to cut existing programs in order to comply with NCLB. A large percentage of educators also feel that NCLB, while effective at identifying failing schools, does little to help them improve student performance.

Although NCLB initially passed through Congress with a majority of votes, many representatives—from both sides of the political spectrum—are now calling for the reform of NCLB. It remains to be seen how this law will develop and how it will continue to impact public schools nationwide. What is certain is that, whatever happens, it will continue to be an influential force in American education.

Education Today

According to Department of Labor statistics, the educational services industry currently employs 13.3 million Americans. This includes employees of public schools, private schools, trade schools and universities. Approximately half of the people in the educational workforce are teachers, while the other half consists of administrators, paraprofessionals, bus drivers, cafeteria workers, social workers and others who contribute to the day-to-day operations of academic institutions.

Education is different from other industries in that the number of job openings is largely determined by fluctuations of the American population, with a greater number of enrolled students resulting in a greater number of job opportunities for educators. (Trends within the education industry may have some impact on the number of jobs available for educators, but in comparison to other industries the effect of industry trends is minimal.) Laws in the United States dictate that all children must attend school until the age of 16. Because of this, the bulk of education positions (63 percent) are in kindergarten through twelfth grade (K-12) environments, with fewer openings at the preschool and post-secondary levels.

In the United States, most K-12 students attend public schools, meaning that there are more professional opportunities in public education than in private education. However, it is difficult to characterize the working conditions for teachers who work in the public education sector because

Visit Vault at **www.vault.com** for insider company profiles, expert advice, career message boards, expert resume reviews, the Vault Job Board and more.

VAULT CAREER LIBRARY

7

these conditions vary enormously, with schools in wealthy communities typically having far greater resources than schools in poor communities.

Demographics

In the past, the majority of teachers were women, particularly at the preschool and elementary levels. Now, at the secondary level, the gender balance is split much more equally. At the elementary level male teachers have become common—although they typically teach the upper elementary school grades. However, despite the overall trend toward a more equal distribution of men and women, kindergarten and preschool teachers are nearly always female. The one area where male teachers are more prevalent than females is postsecondary (university) education, where men comprise about 55 percent of the teaching population.

Job availability

There are thousands of career opportunities for qualified professionals within the field of education. Competition for these positions varies greatly from community to community. Public schools in wealthy suburban communities typically compensate their teachers with generous salaries, and often receive hundreds of applications for every job posting. At the same time, many rural and urban areas are faced with severe teaching shortages and will hire virtually every qualified professional who applies for a job. In fact, districts with severe teaching shortages sometimes hire teachers who are not certified, despite government regulations that prohibit this. Or they may hire teachers to teach "out of license," meaning that the teachers are asked to teach a subject area for which they are not certified.

There are nationwide teaching shortages in math, science and special needs, which means that there is less competition for jobs in these specialty areas. In fact, in some school districts, teachers certified in these high-needs areas may be given special financial incentives to take a job, such as signing bonuses and student loan forgiveness.

Current Trends in Education

CHAPTER 2

Public education is a political hot-button issue at the city, state and federal levels. Politicians regularly clamor for everything from smaller class sizes to merit-based raises for teachers to longer school days. As a result, the policies of public schools across the country are often at the mercy of lawmakers. This leaves many lawmakers—particularly those in low-performance districts, where the changes occur most frequently—feeling as though the curriculum is changed so often that nothing is tried long enough to actually assess whether or not it is successful pedagogy. Educational theories go in and out of style, and school districts often make changes based upon the latest research and ideas about the ways that students learn best. The following pages describe some current trends within the field of education, both those that have been pushed through by politicians and those that represent current thinking among the educational community.

Experiential Learning

Most schools currently favor a hands-on approach to education over the lecture-style lesson format (often referred to as "chalk and talk"). Most current curriculum models at the K-12 levels rely heavily on hands-on activities that allow students to learn through real-life experiences. For example, New York City teachers are currently required to begin each class with a five- or ten-minute mini-lesson that is followed by an extended activity wherein students do work either independently or in small groups, with the teacher circulating the room and assisting students. The teacher then spends the last five minutes of class wrapping up the lesson and soliciting student responses to the activity.

The philosophy of experiential learning dates back to John Dewey, an educational theorist whose vision of progressive education has gone in and out of popularity since the early twentieth century. Dewey believed that students learn best through hands-on experiences. His philosophies also encourage teachers to draw on students' prior knowledge as they introduce students to new concepts—allowing them to make connections between their real-life experiences and concepts covered in the classroom.

The current movement towards hands-on instruction has been gaining momentum since the end of the cold war, after a period of many years when a lecture-based, focus-on-the-basics approach to education was the primary educational model in American schools.

Standardized Testing

The impact of standardized tests on school performance is controversial. In recent years schools around the United States have felt an increasing pressure to raise student test scores.

Impact of NCLB

The No Child Left Behind act magnified the importance of standardized tests by requiring every state to administer annual tests in math and reading to students in third through the eighth grade, in addition to assessing students' progress in science every three years. The stated purpose of this annual testing is that this will ensure that all schools are being held to the same academic standards. However, NCLB allows individual states to design their own tests. In most states the tests are written in the multiple-choice format because this is the cheapest, and most easily measurable type of exam.

Under NCLB, schools are accountable for students' performance on standardized tests. Schools that fail to meet performance benchmarks are labeled as "failing." Critics of NCLB believe that the pressure this puts on schools to raise test scores has created an educational climate where teachers are forced to "teach to the test," rather than spending time on the skills that students most need to learn.

Merit-based pay?

Many politicians believe that individual teachers should be held accountable for their students' performance on standardized tests, with some people suggesting that teacher pay raises should be tied to standardized test scores. This merit-based system of granting teacher pay raises is widely resisted by teachers' unions, which argue that merit-based raises would encourage the best teachers to work in schools that already have high test scores. As a counter to this argument, it has been suggested that a merit-based system might include bonuses or pay raises for teachers in hard-to-staff schools.

Charter Schools

Charter schools are publicly funded schools that are run independently from the local school district. These schools are not required to follow many of the regulations imposed upon other public schools—such as hiring certified teachers. The charter school movement began to gain momentum in the early 1990s, when many states passed laws allowing for their creation.

To form a charter school, a contract (the "charter") must be developed, outlining the goals of the school, and the way its instruction will differ from that of other schools in the area. School charters also typically include a description of how the school's performance goals will be assessed. If a charter school does not meet the goals outlined in the charter, the state department of education may revoke the charter, and the school shut down.

Parents, activists, community leaders or educators who are disillusioned with the quality of public education in their communities may create charter schools. Proponents of charter schools believe that this opportunity for residents of the community to form a school allows the community to participate in the educational process in ways that traditional schools do not.

An alternative to vouchers

Charter schools are frequently viewed as a compromise to the school voucher debate. The movement for vouchers to private schools using funds earmarked for public education is extremely controversial, and strongly opposed by most teachers' unions, educators and political liberals. Charter schools, however, are backed by many politicians on both sides of the political spectrum because they create alternatives to existing public schools without siphoning public school funds to private schools. Instead, they create a new type of public school, while still allowing students to obtain a type of education that could not be provided by the local school district.

The flip side

However, charter schools do have their detractors. Many educators believe that public school funds should stay within the existing public school systems. Furthermore, many people believe that state governments do not adequately monitor charter schools, allowing unsuccessful schools to operate when they are clearly out of compliance with their charters.

Visit Vault at www.vault.com for insider company profiles, expert advice, career message boards, expert resume reviews, the Vault Job Board and more.

VAULT CAREER LIBRARY

11

Failure and success

Research on charter schools has shown mixed results. Some studies indicate that students in charter schools perform better than students in regular public schools, while other studies indicate that their academic performance is worse. In truth, it is difficult to measure the overall effectiveness of charter schools because these schools utilize such a wide range of missions, philosophies and pedagogical techniques. The majority of charter schools fail within 18 months, but there are also many that have been extremely successful. One highly-thought-of group of charter schools is KIPP (Knowledge is Power Program) Academy. These charter schools were created by Teach for America alumni and have been very successful in neighborhoods that are notorious for their low-performing public schools, and they are now located throughout the country.

The Small School Movement

In recent years, there has been a movement in big cities towards breaking up large schools into smaller learning communities. The thinking behind this is that students, particularly those in high-needs, low-income areas, perform better in small settings, where teachers and other adults can get to know each student personally. In most cases, these new, small schools are located within large buildings, where one large school has been broken up and replaced by several smaller schools, each with its own administration.

School systems with small schools often allow students to choose a school that fits their academic interests—particularly at the high school level. For example, students may choose a school that emphasizes journalism, the health professions or the sciences, allowing them to focus on the academic areas they are most interested in, and encouraging them to think about their long-term career goals.

While the small school movement has had proponents for many years, it is only in recent years that large school systems have seriously begun to replace "mega-schools" with smaller learning communities. This is due largely to funding by the Bill and Melinda Gates foundation, which has given many millions of dollars to school systems across the country for the purpose of creating small schools. At this time, it appears that the small school movement has been largely successful; students in smaller schools tend to perform better than those in enormous schools, and teachers in small schools frequently feel that they have more support from their administration and more of a say in the operations of the school.

Corporate Sponsorship and Private Grants

In recent years, corporate sponsorships have played a significant role in American education. Often, corporate sponsorships fund specific academic programs. For example, the *Detroit Free Press* sponsors high school journalism programs in Detroit, and JP Morgan Chase sponsors a business mentoring program in New York City. Organizations such as these are willing to fund academic programs as a way of contributing to their communities and creating good public relations. And most educators welcome this type of corporate sponsorship.

Funding controversy

Other corporate sponsorships are more controversial. Fast food companies have donated money to schools across the country in exchange for permission to place advertisements in school cafeterias. An article, *Junk Food Companies Market to Kids at School*, published on abc.com estimates that 67 percent of public school children in America see fast food advertisements at school. With growing concerns about childhood obesity and nutrition, many see this type of advertising as encouraging unhealthy behavior in a way that that is inappropriate within the school environment.

Despite the controversies, a growing number of school systems across the country actively seek funding from corporate sponsors. These include both low-income schools that need funding for basic academic programs and schools in wealthy areas that hope to create opportunities for academic enrichment.

In addition to corporate sponsorship, there are many grants available for school programs. The Bill and Melinda Gates Foundation—the largest charitable trust in the world—spends a great deal of its resources on public education in America, and has become an extremely influential force. However, this is only one of many organizations dedicated to funding public education programs in the United States. Teachers and administrators who take the time to seek out grant money are often rewarded.

Visit Vault at **www.vault.com** for insider company profiles, expert advice, career message boards, expert resume reviews, the Vault Job Board and more.

VAULT CAREER LIBRARY

13

Increased Emphasis on World Languages

For many years, instruction in world languages was typically limited to Spanish, French and German at the secondary level. In recent years, however, many schools have adopted international curricula that place an increased emphasis on world languages. At the elementary school level, this often means teaching an international language (typically Spanish) in the early grades—breaking away from the educational model in which instruction in world languages is reserved for secondary students. And at the secondary level, many schools now offer instruction in languages that until recently were reserved for students at the university level, such as Chinese, Japanese and Arabic. This trend is a result of globalization and the growing influence of international business. With many companies desperate for employees who are fluent in multiple languages, schools increasingly view language studies as a critical factor in preparing students for professional success.

Different Types of Schools

CHAPTER 3

There are many different kinds of public schools and many different types of private schools. Both types of schools encompass a wide range of educational philosophies, student demographics and operating budgets. And a public school in one area might offer the type and style of education that is more typical of private schools in another area. Therefore, it is difficult to make generalizations about the characteristics of public schools or private schools. At the same time, because public schools are funded with government money, there are certain differences between the two types of schools. These are described on the following pages.

Public Schools

All public schools are funded by taxpayers' money. In many cases, these funds come from federal, state and city governments—and as a result, the federal, state and city governments have the authority to oversee the educational process of public schools.

In the past, the federal government was less involved in public education, but with the No Child Left Behind Act, this has changed. Public schools are now under an immense amount of pressure from the federal government to raise standardized test scores. This is something that many educators are unhappy with, because they do not view multiple-choice exams as a comprehensive means of student assessment. The impact of NCLB has been felt in every public school in the country, although this pressure is particularly intense in schools that are labeled as failing. In addition to the pressures from NCLB, many state governments will also take drastic measures with schools that fail to improve their test scores. These measures may include replacing the school administration, implementing a scripted curriculum or closing down the school entirely.

Regulations stipulate that all public teachers be certified (or in the case of alternative certification programs, in the process of completing the certification process). In some school districts, local authorities may also require schools to follow a certain curriculum or pedagogical philosophy, and schools considered failing are more likely to have curricula imposed upon them than high performing public schools.

Unions

Virtually all public school teachers belong to unions. This is one reason why compensation and benefits packages for public school employees are so carefully regulated, with most school systems paying teachers according to a pay scale. Teachers' unions also help determining the maximum number of students that may be placed in a classroom. When there are reports of class-size violations, teachers unions may send representatives to investigate the situations, and file grievances against the school administration if necessary.

Tenure

Public schools also typically follow a tenure system, meaning that after teachers have worked in the district for several years, they cannot be fired unless in serious violation of district rules. This is an advantage for teachers because it gives them a large degree of job security—and prevents districts from laying off experienced teachers to hire people lower on the pay scale. At the same time, many people interested in educational reform feel that the tenure system prevents school systems from finding the best, most qualified teachers to work in their schools.

Serving the community

Public schools are required to accept all students who live in the community. Therefore, in most areas, the population of the public schools is representative of the community at large. Public schools are also required to provide special needs services to the students who need them. (Although not every individual school will provide every type of special needs service. When this is the case, students may need to travel to a school that does offer the required services and the district will provide transportation.)

While many people are critical about the state of public education, there are legions of fantastic public schools in the United States. And, although government involvement can be a source of frustration, a career in public education offers a great deal of job security, guaranteed pay increases and other types of stability that are appealing to many professionals. In addition, many educators have a strong belief in the importance of public education and a dedication to working in a public school environment.

Private Schools

Because private schools are funded privately, they aren't bound by many of the mandates that affect public schools, and the No Child Left Behind Act has had very little impact on private schools. In fact, private schools are not even required to administer standardized tests (although many of them choose to do so as a way of assessing student progress). Private schools also have a great deal of freedom to choose their own curricula and to teach in accordance to whatever educational philosophy they advocate.

Despite the fact that private schools are permitted to develop their own curricula, most private schools are influenced by the curriculum requirements for public schools in their states—although they are not required to do so. For example, seventh grade math students in Florida public schools are expected to learn how to find the area of a circle—and it is therefore likely that a private school in Florida will teach this information to seventh graders as well. By using state curriculum guidelines as the base for their own curricula, private schools make it easier for students to transition from public schools to private schools, and vice versa.

Parochial schools

In parochial schools, those private schools that are affiliated with a religious institution, religion may be a part of the school's day-to-day instruction. Many parochial schools have daily religion courses, and students may be required to attend religious services. In conjunction with this, political issues in a private school may be discussed in a way that would be unacceptable in a public school. (For example, an issue such as abortion might be discussed in a way that emphasizes a particular viewpoint.)

The role of religion within parochial schools varies widely, even within schools associated with a particular religious denomination. For example, many Catholic schools have large numbers of non-Catholic students in attendance, and include very little religious education in their curricula. In other Catholic schools, students may be expected to attend daily religion classes and weekly mass and daily prayer sessions.

Many parochial school teachers believe that religious instruction is an important part of a well-rounded education. Other teachers believe that religion should not have any role in an academic environment at all. And many others fall somewhere in between. Certainly, before obtaining a job in a parochial school, teachers should make an effort to learn about the role that religious education plays a part in the school, and how they will be

Visit Vault at www.vault.com for insider company profiles, expert advice, career message boards, expert resume reviews, the Vault Job Board and more.

VAULT CAREER LIBRARY   17

expected to reinforce this aspect of students' education. It is essential that all teachers in parochial schools support and accept the role of religion within the school, whatever that role may be.

Benefactors

While private schools do not face the government mandates and restrictions of public schools, they rely on private funding and often find themselves beholden to their benefactors. In some cases, they may be forced to adapt their curricula to the whims and desires of the people who donate large amounts of money to the school. While a good private school will put limits on the types of decisions that benefactors are allowed to make, the need for donations is a reality in almost any private school. Teachers in private schools may also feel pressured by parents who feel that if they pay large sums of money toward their child's education, their child should then be able to get into a certain college, perform advanced academic tasks or even be guaranteed certain grades. Again, a good private school will support its teachers if faced with unreasonable parents, but this can still be an uncomfortable dynamic.

Certification not required

Private schools are not required to hire certified teachers, although most private schools do require that their teachers be certified. In some cases, however, particularly at the secondary level, experience in a given field may be viewed as preferable to formal teacher training. For example, a private school might hire a native speaker of German or Spanish to teach in the international languages department, instead of a certified teacher. Or they might hire a reporter from the local newspaper to teach a journalism course.

Job stability

Teachers in private schools often do not have the support and protection of a teacher's union. (Although in large cities, certain groups of private schools such as Catholic schools may have their own unions.) Thus, private school teachers tend to have less job stability than teachers in public schools and usually do not work on the tenure system. This means that, theoretically, a teacher in a private school might be fired without warning because of an argument with an administrator or a complaint from a parent. This is a rare occurrence, but it is something that private school teachers are more vulnerable to than are public school teachers.

Lower salaries

Teacher salaries in private schools are typically much lower than in public schools. In fact, the average public school teacher makes 61 percent more than the average private school teacher. There are some elite private schools that pay their teachers well, but in many cases, the more elite the school, the lower the teacher salaries will be. (But if a school is boarding as opposed to just day, a teacher's room and/or board may also be covered.) One reason for the low salaries is that many teachers are willing to work for less money in a school where they believe students will be motivated, academically talented and well-behaved.

Student demographics

Private schools are entitled to enroll whichever students they want. (Although anti-discrimination laws do apply to private schools; meaning that they cannot refuse to admit students based on their race or ethnicity if they accept public funding of any kind.) Some private schools will only enroll students who are among the top students in their community. Others may have open enrollments, while declining to accept students who need special needs services that they do not have the resources to provide.

Often, private schools have smaller class sizes than public schools and many see this as an advantage of private education. However, at the same time, class sizes in private schools are not regulated. This means that some private schools—particularly those with lower tuitions—have class sizes that are significantly larger than those found in the public school system.

Tuition and scholarships

Because private schools charge tuition, students in these schools tend to be from higher socioeconomic groups than other children in the community. This is particularly true of elite private schools that have higher tuitions than most universities. As a result, private schools may have more homogenous student bodies than public schools. If the tuition is expensive, then the student body may be made up largely of children of the wealthy. If the academic standards are strict, it follows that all of the students admitted will be bright.

While a school filled with bright children is looked upon favorably by most people, a school filled with wealthy children is considered less desirable because many educators believe in the value of providing students with exposure to people from different backgrounds. Therefore, in an effort to diversify their student bodies, and to provide opportunities for children

Visit Vault at **www.vault.com** for insider company profiles, expert advice, career message boards, expert resume reviews, the Vault Job Board and more.

VAULT CAREER LIBRARY

19

from poor families, most private schools offer scholarships to a certain percentage of students. And often it's the most elite private schools that offer the greatest number of scholarships, since these schools' endowments enable them to comfortably do so.

Are Private Schools better than Public Schools?

Some people firmly believe in the benefits of public education and in the philosophy of providing a free education to everyone. Others believe that private schools have higher academic standards and offer a superior education. In truth, there are both great public schools and great private schools. At the same time, there are both inadequate public schools and inadequate private schools. In fact, recent studies have shown that, with a control for socioeconomic status, private school and public school students perform equally on standardized tests, which indicates that the differences are not as great as many people believe they are.

Many teachers gravitate towards private schools because they believe that students in the private-school environment are better behaved than those in the public schools. Often, this is the case, in large part because private schools have the authority to expel any student whose behavior is consistently inappropriate. However, despite this, there are private schools with chronic behavior problems, and a teacher who lacks classroom management skills is likely to have problems in even the most elite academic environments.

When applying for teaching jobs, you should consider the advantages and disadvantages of both public and private education. If you have a strong preference for one type of school over the other, that's fine. If not, you should look at all the schools in your area—both public and private—and then apply to whichever schools will best meet your needs as an educator.

Goals and Responsibilities of an Educator

CHAPTER 4

Educating Students

The principal responsibility of an educator is to give students skills and information. This involves creating lessons and activities that teach students concepts that are appropriate for their developmental stage, and that comply with any curriculum guidelines imposed by the school or school district.

In K-12, education teachers are expected to apply "differentiated instruction" in the classroom. This refers to teaching one concept through a variety of different activities that allow students to absorb information in different ways. For example, a teacher might discuss a scientific concept such as gravity by giving a short lecture using visual diagrams, performing a demonstration, and having students perform a scientific experiment. Educational research suggests that some students learn best through listening, others through visual information, and yet others through hands-on experience. In an effort to educate students with different learning styles, teachers are encouraged—and often required—to reinforce important concepts through a variety of different activities. Differentiated instruction also requires teachers to tailor lessons and activities to students with different abilities and skill levels. This is especially important when special needs students and ELL students are in integrated into the classroom.

Advocacy for Students' Well-Being

In addition to caring for children's academic needs, teachers (particularly those working at the K-12 level) are expected to identify students who are coping with social and emotional problems outside of school. These problems may include neglect, social maladjustment, academic pressure from parents, abuse, eating disorders, depression and drug use. Teachers are expected to refer students to a school counselor or social worker when they recognize signs of a serious problem.

Going the extra mile

Many teachers go the extra mile for students who are in need. For example, a teacher might purchase shoes for a child whose family can't afford them, or simply spend time after school listening to a student who is upset about an argument with a friend. These things are not in the official job description of a classroom teacher, yet many teachers feel that it is their responsibility to do whatever they can to ensure the happiness and well-being of their students.

Reporting abuse

Whenever teachers have any suspicion that a child is being physically or sexually abused, they are required by law to report this to local child welfare agencies. In most cases, a teacher will first report suspicions of abuse to a school administrator or counselor who will file the actual report to the authorities. However, if the school administration is unwilling to report suspected abuse, the teacher is under legal obligation to file a report if he or she continues to believe that abuse is taking place. Educators and certain other "mandated reporters" (such as therapists) are under greater legal obligation to report child abuse than the average person. When teachers fail to report child abuse, they risk facing hefty fines, or even jail time. This is evidence of the responsibility our society places on educators for ensuring the welfare of school-aged children.

Lesson Planning

Teachers are expected to be well prepared, with written lesson plans that detail the day's activities. Some schools require teachers to submit lessons on a daily or weekly basis. Other schools simply expect teachers to have lesson plans available upon request. A lesson plan should have enough detail to demonstrate that the day's activities were well thought out, engaging, and in line with the school curriculum.

Mandated curriculum

Some schools have a mandated lesson plan format and "scripted curriculum," while others leave planning largely to the teacher's discretion. The advantage of a scripted curriculum is that it takes much of the time out of lesson planning. The disadvantage is that many teachers feel that it takes the creativity out of the lesson planning process. Furthermore, if a scripted curriculum is not in line with the academic needs of the students, it may be difficult to adapt the lessons without deviating from the school's curriculum mandates. For example, teachers in low-performing schools often find that the stories in the required textbook are at a reading level that is much more advanced than that of the students in their classrooms.

College-level

At the university level, teachers are rarely required to have formal lesson plans, although many of them do prepare detailed lectured notes for each class they teach. Professors are also typically required to present a syllabus or course outline to their supervisors before the beginning of each academic term. This syllabus is typically given to students during the first week of class to give students an understanding of the scope of the course and the assignments they will be expected to complete.

Paperwork

Most teachers spend an enormous amount of time completing paperwork. This includes time spent grading papers, which can be incredibly time-consuming, particularly at the higher grade levels. In addition, they are expected to keep anecdotal records of student behavior. These "anecdotals" may be used as evidence if a school decides to place a student in a special needs classroom, or to take dramatic disciplinary action. Teachers also keep attendance records, and are expected to notify the administration if a student is chronically truant. Teachers who work with special needs students are required to keep detailed records of their daily interactions with students, and the steps that were taken to meet the needs of each student, as specified by their individual education plans (IEPs).

Communicating with Parents and Caregivers

In addition to establishing a positive rapport with students, teachers are expected to be in contact with parents and other caregivers, such as grandparents or foster parents. Most schools have several parent/teacher conference days scattered throughout the school year, but teacher contact with parents is expected to extend beyond this. Teachers should call, e-mail, or write notes to parents on a regular basis. Communication with parents should include information about students' achievements as well as

Visit Vault at **www.vault.com** for insider company profiles, expert advice, career message boards, expert resume reviews, the Vault Job Board and more.

VAULT CAREER LIBRARY   23

any areas for concern. If there are serious problems concerning a student's behavior or academic development, a meeting may be scheduled with the parent or caregiver, and possibly a school administrator or counselor. It's crucial that caregivers be up-to-date on their child's progress, particularly if the student's behavior or academic performance is unsatisfactory. A successful K-12 teacher will create productive relationships with students' caregivers, treating them as members of a team that is working together to ensure the student's success.

Different Types of Teaching Careers

CHAPTER 5

The most important things to determine when preparing for a career in education are the age of the students you would like to work with, and whether you want to teach in a public or private school. If you decide to teach at the secondary or post-secondary level, you will also need to specialize in one or more academic subject areas. The next few pages examine these different work settings within the field of education. As you will see, the field of education offers a wide range of career opportunities.

Public Schools

More than 90 percent of K-12 students in the United States attend public schools. Working conditions in public schools vary greatly, depending on the financial resources of the community, the school administration and the regulations imposed upon schools by city and state authorities. Public schools may receive funding from federal, state and city governments, although much of the federal education funding is earmarked for programs that serve children in high-needs areas where school resources are limited and academic performance is below average.

In many regions of the country, school districts receive funding that comes from local millage taxes. These taxes are paid by residents of a community in order to fund educational programs in their city; residents agree to these millage tax increases through local elections. Wealthy communities often have significant millage taxes that result in well-funded schools with high teacher salaries, extra-curricular programs, arts education, and other programs that schools in poorer areas cannot afford. Occasionally, a community will vote to discontinue a pre-existing millage tax. When this occurs, school districts are often forced to downsize staff, cut back educational programs and otherwise reduce their operating costs.

Private and Parochial Schools

Private schools are largely funded by tuition payments, with added financial support from alumni and others who support the school. Although television shows and movies often depict private schools as places with rigorous academic standards and students from mega-wealthy families, there are also private schools dedicated to serving poor and middle-class students. In large cities there are a small number of exclusive private schools with extravagant tuitions—schools where a year of kindergarten is more expensive than a year in an Ivy League university—but the majority of private schools are far more modest. In fact, the demographics of private school students are nearly as diverse as they are in public schools.

Religious affiliations

A large percentage of private schools are affiliated with religious organizations. These schools are known as parochial schools. Some parochial schools include a great deal of religious training in their curricula, while others have a multi-faith population of students and put little emphasis on religion. Catholic schools, which make up a large percentage of the parochial schools in the United States, often require students to take religious courses and attend Catholic mass, but very rarely require that students be Catholic to attend the school.

Parochial schools in low-income areas are sometimes funded largely by church-affiliated organizations, offering students a subsidized tuition rate so that they can obtain a private school education at relatively low cost. And these types of parochial schools often have high academic standards, although they may not have the resources of more expensive private schools. In fact, in many urban areas, private schools often have larger class sizes than public schools, where teachers' unions regulate the maximum number of students in a class.

Private school myths

Contrary to what many people believe, private schools often pay teachers much less than public schools. This is due in part to the high level of competition for teaching positions in private schools. The commonly held belief that private school students are well-behaved and academically inclined fuels the competition for teaching positions in private schools, meaning that these schools can get away with paying their teachers less. Furthermore, some private schools, particularly those in low-income areas, have limited budgets; this may result in very low teacher salaries. For example, teachers in New York City Catholic schools earn about half the salaries of NYC public school teachers.

Academic Specialty Areas

Elementary

At the elementary level, one teacher typically teaches all of the major subject areas: math, science, language arts, and social studies (although in schools with low standardized test scores, students may travel to a specialized math class). Elementary students do typically travel to another classroom and another teacher for instruction in music, art, and physical education.

When students reach middle school they begin to travel between teachers and classrooms, attending classes with teachers who have specialized training in different content areas, such as math, language arts and science.

Secondary

At the high school level, the subject areas become more specific. For example, a certified science teacher may teach biology, chemistry, or earth science; a math teacher might teach algebra, calculus, or geometry; and an English teacher might teach composition, British literature, or American literature.

Teachers at the secondary level are required to specialize in one subject area. Many teachers choose to specialize in the subject area (or areas) where they have the greatest personal interest. Others specialize in high-needs subject areas such as math and science to increase their odds of being hired by a competitive school district.

Specialized assistance

Most schools have pull-out teachers who provide instruction to small groups of students who need specialized assistance. Literacy specialists work with students whose reading and writing skills are below grade level. Resource room teachers work with students who have learning disabilities and need specialized academic support. English language learning (ELL) teachers work with students whose first language is something other than English. (In the past, ELL instruction was commonly referred to as ESL— or English as a second language—but this terminology is currently out of

Visit Vault at **www.vault.com** for insider company profiles, expert advice, career message boards, expert resume reviews, the Vault Job Board and more.

VAULT CAREER LIBRARY

27

vogue in American education.) Speech therapists work with students who have speech difficulties, including students whose difficulties with speech are due to hearing difficulties.

The ability to specialize in a specific content area is, for many people, an attractive aspect of a career in education. Educators have the opportunity to share their knowledge of the topics they are most passionate about on a daily basis. Teachers of the arts are particularly drawn to education for this reason, because there are few other fields that will allow them to dedicate their workdays to the creation of art or music.

Other Roles in the School Setting

In addition to classroom teachers, there are other education professionals who fill distinct roles within the school setting.

Media specialists

Media specialists work with students in the school library. No longer simply filling the role of librarian, media specialists help students find information using both old and new technologies. At the elementary level, the media specialist introduces students to the features of a library, reads stories to the class and helps students develop an appreciation for books. As students enter the secondary level, library visits focus more on research strategies, and class visits are scheduled at the classroom teacher's discretion. In addition to working with entire classes, media specialists regularly assist students who visit the library independently, either to find information for a school project or out of personal interest.

School counselors

School counselors work with students who have a wide range of social and emotional difficulties. In some cases, students visit a school counselor to help cope with traumatic events at home, such as divorce, serious illness of a parent, or a history of abuse and neglect. Other students visit the school counselor simply because they need coaching to help further their social skills (such as the kindergartener who has problems sharing). The school counselor often acts a mediator in conflicts between students, and in this role frequently meets with small groups of two or more students. Additionally, counselors routinely visit classrooms to teach lessons. At the lower grade levels, this might involve talking to classes about topics such as bullying, friendship, and anger management. At the high school level, a counselor is likely to teach lessons on topics such as the college admissions process.

School social workers

School social workers, like counselors, spend their time working with students who have personal and/or academic problems. Social workers, however, often work with families of students as well, conducting home visits on a regular basis. In situations where a child does not have enough food, clothing or adequate living conditions due to economic need, the social worker may help the child's family connect with government and nonprofit organizations that can address these needs. Social workers also spend a great deal of time working with special needs students. This involves helping family members understand the child's disabilities, and ensuring that the child's academic needs are met. School social workers work with special needs teachers to create an individual education plan (IEP) for all special needs students. These plans typically contain a list of specific academic goals for the child, the means by which these goals will be achieved and the assessment tools that will be used to assess the student's progress. Because IEPs for special needs students are heavily regulated, most school social workers spend a significant amount of time filling out paperwork in addition to working directly with children and their families.

K-12 administrators

K-12 school administrators hire and supervise teachers, oversee the implementation of curriculum, deal with serious disciplinary problems, and manage the overall operations of the school. In small schools, the administration may be limited to the school principal. In larger schools— including most secondary schools—the administrative team usually also includes one or more vice principles and deans. At the high school level, department chairs often oversee the academic initiatives in a specific subject area.

Other Education-Related Careers

At the university level, there are many different types of administrative positions, for example the admissions department (which selects the students who will be admitted to a specific college or program) and the communications department (which writes and designs letters, brochures, catalogs and websites for students, prospective students and alumni). Study abroad programs, lecture series and myriad other university programs also have administrative staff members who are responsible for executing the goals of the program and providing support to students and faculty members.

There are also companies that publish books, design software and create other educational tools for use in the classroom. These organizations often have a staff that includes trained educators as well as writers, designers, marketing specialists and business professionals.

GETTING HIRED

Teacher Education and Certification

CHAPTER 6

The Traditional Path

For many years, the vast majority of teachers entered the workforce immediately after completing a four-year degree in education, and to this day, the majority of teachers enter the field of education by following this path. The traditional way to becoming a teacher involves following a typical liberal arts curriculum supplemented with extensive coursework in education, as well as content area specialization for people who plan to teach at the secondary level.

Undergraduate education

Undergraduate education curricula usually require students to spend significant amounts of time (or "observation hours") in different types of schools throughout their undergraduate training. After completing most of their coursework, teachers-in-training become student teachers, an experience that involves working in a classroom with a successful, experienced teacher. Student teachers usually begin by observing the class and then take on greater amounts of teaching, grading and lesson planning activities during the student teaching semester.

Certification

Public school teachers at the K-12 level must be certified by the state in which they teach. The traditional teaching certification process involves extensive coursework at the undergraduate level, and a semester of student teaching. In addition, all states now require teachers to pass one or more standardized tests to become certified. Teachers are also typically required to attend seminars on recognizing and reporting child abuse, and to pass a criminal background check as a part of the teacher certification process. Many states also require teachers to take courses and attend seminars throughout their careers in order to maintain their certification.

Most states use a tiered certification system that requires teachers to complete numerous tasks in order to reach the final level of certification, something that usually occurs after several years in the classroom. Basically, this means that even though in some states teachers become certified after completing college and passing their teacher exams, this certification is still provisional in many states. To receive a more permanent level of certification, teachers may have to earn additional academic credits, prove themselves in the classroom or pass another practical exam after several years of teaching. For example, a teacher straight out of an undergraduate program might receive a temporary or provisional certificate that lasts for several years, but be required to pass an exam and complete graduate-level coursework before being given a 'permanent' certificate.

Test preparation

Most states use a uniform test called the PRAXIS. PRAXIS I covers general knowledge, and PRAXIS II covers material related to specific content area. Several states use their own standardized tests instead of the PRAXIS; these states are California, Colorado, Florida, Georgia, Illinois, Massachusetts, Michigan, New York, Tennessee, Virginia and Washington.

People right out of college with strong academic backgrounds typically have little trouble passing their teacher exams. If someone is taking the exams years after completing college, or otherwise looking for extra preparation, there are plenty of books and exam prep programs available; for example, Kaplan teaches prep courses for PRAXIS and other U.S. teacher training programs.

State reciprocity

The NASDTEC Interstate Agreement Facilitating Mobility of Educational Personnel allows for reciprocity in teaching certification between different states. This makes it easier for a teacher who is certified in one state to teach in another. Some states, however, do not participate in NASDTEC (the National Assocation of State Directors of Teacher Education and Certification). And some participating states may require teachers to fulfill minor requirements, such as taking a standardized test or completing a course, in order to transfer their certification. States that do not participate in the general reciprocity agreement will, in most cases, give some credit to teachers from other states for completed coursework, practical experiences, and other requirements that count toward certification.

States participating in the NASDTEC teacher certification reciprocity agreement:

Alabama	Mississippi
Arkansas	Montana
Arizona	Nevada*
California	New Mexico
Colorado	North Carolina
Connecticut*	Ohio
Delaware*	Oklahoma
District of Columbia	Oregon*
Florida*	Rhode Island
Georgia	South Carolina*
Hawaii	South Dakota*
Idaho	Tennessee
Indiana	Texas
Kansas	Utah*
Kentucky	Vermont*
Louisiana	Virginia
Maine	Washington
Maryland*	West Virginia
Massachusetts*	Wyoming
Michigan	

* States marked with asterisks do not accept teaching certificates from every other state participating in NASDTEC. Also note that non-participating states may have independent reciprocity agreements with other states.

Visit Vault at www.vault.com for insider company profiles, expert advice, career message boards, expert resume reviews, the Vault Job Board and more.

VAULT CAREER LIBRARY

35

Exceptions to Certification

Private schools

Private schools and charter schools are not required to employ certified teachers. They might, for example, hire a native French speaker to teach French classes rather than a certified French teacher. However, in most cases they do require their teachers to be certified as a condition of employment.

Higher education

At the higher education level, professors are usually not required to have completed any formal training in education, although most hiring committees do consider teaching experience—such as working as a teaching assistant while in graduate school—to be a plus. Four-year colleges usually require professors to have a PhD in their academic specialty area (or the terminal degree in the field being taught, such as a JD in the case of law professors, and an MD for medical school professors). In most cases, colleges and universities also seek job candidates who have published books or articles in scholarly journals, or who have made significant achievements in their field (for example, art professors are usually successful artists who have had their work shown in galleries and museums).

Two-year community colleges often have much looser requirements for their professors than four-year universities. Debbie Beaudin, who taught at the community college level for several years says, "I was an adjunct professor of a remedial writing class. To do this you needed a bachelor's, not a masters, so it was perfect."

Advantages to Traditional Certification

The traditional path to certification has the advantage of giving students solid preparation for a career in education, including extensive time working with students. Steve Tullin, a veteran teacher and staff developer who followed the traditional pathway into education, says that the "number one advantage of traditional certification is that you enter the field with the mindset that this is what you want to do. You don't feel like you have as many alternatives. I think that this is an advantage because it keeps you on track with respect to having a goal, and gives you a commitment to staying the course with the teaching profession."

A traditional, undergraduate education program in education also has the advantage of getting teachers out into the classroom at an early stage in their training. Rachel Wadle, an early education teacher in Iowa says, "In the first year I was already taking my education classes. I was in the classroom and experiencing the kids. I didn't sit in class the whole first two years doing electives."

Especially if you're young

Another advantage of the traditional pathway into education is that it allows undergraduate students who are in school full time to complete their education requirements before they are full-time members of the workforce. High school English teacher Brigid Tileston says, "A big advantage is being able to do your clinical or observation hours while you're an undergrad and you have more time. Trying to work in your observation hours while working 40 hours a week in another job can be kind of tricky. Plus, you're given more time to do your student teaching; time where you're able to train with a veteran, experienced teacher. In a master's program you might have only 10 weeks. When you have more time you're able to learn a lot from an experienced teacher, and it gives you the chance to make certain mistakes early on. Not that you can't do a great job if you do it another way, but it's harder. With undergraduate training you are being educated in a more supported environment."

The traditional path to certification is ideal for people who make the decision to become teachers at a young age. Betsy Sullivan, a career teacher and counselor says, "I don't remember ever not wanting to be a teacher. My grandmother was a teacher and as I child I listened to her stories and always wanted to do that." However, in the modern workforce it is common for people to change careers, and education has an especially strong appeal for career changers because of its altruistic qualities and because working in a school is often attractive to people who want to escape the corporate office environment. As a result, it is becoming more common for career changers to become certified teachers through other routes.

Master's Degrees with Certification Programs

Most universities now offer masters' with certification programs in education. These programs are designed for career changers who possess a college degree in a subject other than education. This degree (unlike master's programs for people who are already teachers) prepares students for teacher certification. Master's with certification programs, like traditional certification programs, require students to take extensive coursework in addition to spending time student teaching (although the student teaching experience is often shortened—to eight or 10 weeks rather than an entire semester). Many universities offer master's with certification courses in the evening so that career changers can continue to work full-time jobs while completing their education coursework. In most cases, however, students in these programs must quit their full-time jobs before student teaching because of scheduling conflicts and the demanding nature of the student teaching experience.

Higher pay...

Because the pay scales of most public school systems determine teacher salaries by years of experience and the teacher's own level of education education, teachers who become certified through a master's program begin their teaching careers at a higher pay grade than those who become certified through the traditional undergraduate route.

Clara Lin, an elementary school teacher who became certified through a master's with certification program, says that this was preferable to the traditional route for her because, "I just didn't know when I was eighteen years old exactly what I wanted to do. Although I did think that I wanted to teach, I wasn't sure at what level and wasn't willing to devote my entire undergraduate education to something I wasn't sure about."

Although stressful, some people who pursue master's degrees while working full time find that the experience of working and studying has advantages. Casie Smith found a job as a preschool teacher after finishing an undergraduate degree in developmental psychology. Preschool teachers are not typically required to have a degree in education, but she decided to pursue a master's while continuing to teach three days a week. "As much as you can learn through theory, you can learn more through experience in the classroom working with the kids," she says. "It's better than going into someone else's classroom and working with their lesson plans. I found that I had a better understanding of the theories we were talking about because I could think of real life examples. So rather than having to separate learning from experience it was nice to be able to do it all at once. It's not easy to work and go to school full time, but I felt like I got more out of it because I was already in the classroom."

...but more expensive for employers

Although a master's with certification program offers many of the benefits of undergraduate training, some people who complete these programs find it difficult to land a first job. Because teachers with master's degrees are higher on teacher pay scales than teachers straight out of undergraduate schools, competitive school districts will often choose to hire the cheaper candidate if they have a choice—especially when neither candidate has previous experience. In fact some school districts will not accept applications from teachers with master's degrees and no prior teaching experience. Note that this is not the case in large, urban districts that desperately need teachers, but it is something that someone who wants to teach in a competitive suburban district should be aware of.

This was the case for Jim Tileston, who eventually found a teaching position at a Catholic school in suburban Chicago. "When you finish a master's program with no teaching experience, you're at a major disadvantage because of economic situations," he says. "This is something that no graduate school is going to teach you. My advice for someone in undergrad would be to get the certification then, because in the environment we're in now, with the economy in many districts they will not hire someone with a master's and limited experience. I'm competing with people who have an undergrad bachelor's degree and certification. Because of pay scale they could pay another guy significantly less. It's a no-brainer from an administrative standpoint. No one's valuing my age or professional experience; I didn't find that out until it was way too late. However, my understanding is that after three years of experience the master's does become way more valuable. At that point it comes down to your classroom experience and skills as a teacher. But right now most of the school districts in my area have a moratorium for people with my qualifications."

At the same time, Jim feels that he benefited from getting his teacher training after several years of experience in another field. "I entered the teaching profession with much greater maturity, drive and a sense of focus. I also had a better understanding of the political climate we're in and the way the world really works. This helped me get a lot more out of my classes. When I was an undergrad I blew off some of my classes, but by waiting to get my teacher certification I really took school seriously and got every bit out of the classes that I could."

Visit Vault at **www.vault.com** for insider company profiles, expert advice, career message boards, expert resume reviews, the Vault Job Board and more.

V/\ULT CAREER LIBRARY

39

It's also worth noting that while it may be more difficult for people who follow the master's with education track to break into the field of education in certain areas, the disadvantages of this pathway typically disappear once a teacher has gained several years of experience in the classroom.

Alternative Certification Programs

The desire of many people to enter the field of education as career changers, combined with severe teaching shortages in many school districts has resulted in the formation of dozens of teacher certification programs that are widely known as "alternative certification programs." These programs offer people who do not possess teacher certification or formal training to enter the classroom under the condition that they work towards obtaining the necessary credentials. Typically, members of alternative teacher certification programs are placed in schools that are "hard to staff." This euphemism usually refers to schools in low-income neighborhoods. However, Debbie Beaudin, a high school teacher who began her career as a member of the New York City Teaching Fellows—one of the nation's largest alternative certification programs—warns against equating low-income neighborhoods with high-needs schools. "When I think of a high needs school, I think of a school that is neglected. There are a lot of schools in low-income areas that are excellent schools. It's not the population that you teach that makes it a high needs school," she says.

Running the gamut

Alternative certification programs vary dramatically in their scope, complexity and the level of support they offer to members of their programs. Many cities and states around the country will often allow people with bachelor's degrees to enter the classroom if they enroll in a teacher-training program, without providing participants with any additional training or support. Other programs, such as Teach for America, have rigorous entry requirements and require program members to enroll in master's degree programs tailored to the needs of people who are placed as teachers in difficult environments with minimal formal training.

Advantages

There is not clear consensus on how effective alternative certification programs are. Certainly, these programs have many advantages. As previously mentioned, they have been a successful means of filling teaching shortages in some of the most challenged school districts in the country. And although the members of these programs enter the field without much training, they enter the teaching profession with a commitment to complete their training and fulfill all other requirements for certification within a specified amount of time, usually two or three years. Furthermore, large alternative certification programs such as Teach for America and the New York City Teaching Fellows programs give career changers access to a subsidized master's program, which makes entering the field of education more financially feasible to many would-be career changers.

Debbie Beaudin says that she was initially attracted to the Teaching Fellows Program because "I knew they would help me with the red tape, and that they would help me get a master's. I didn't know how I would get a master's if I stayed at my old job. I knew that it was possible but I didn't know how I would do it."

Chad Hamilton, who also completed the New York City Teaching Fellows program, became interested in teaching while working towards a master's degree in art at New York University. "I was recruited to volunteer with a program called America Reads. Through this program, college students go to high-needs schools and tutor kids in reading and math. I did this in Bed Stuy [a neighborhood in Brooklyn] with first and second graders. At the end of two years, I'd developed a relationship with people at the school— they really liked me and recommended that I look into the Teaching Fellows. I started looking at the Fellows as my graduate school program came to an end, and as I started thinking about how to make money. On some level it was a practical decision: this was something I could get into that was really stable for someone with an art school degree. I also enjoyed working with the kids so much that it seemed like the right thing to do."

Many alternative certification programs are very selective in choosing candidates for their programs. As a result, they bring people who are intelligent, well-educated and successful into the education field. Steve Tullin, a staff developer who has mentored numerous members of the New York City Teaching Fellows alternative certification program, says, "There are tremendous advantages with Fellows. The program has set up certain criteria to get in. I believe that they require a 3.5 undergraduate grade point average, and right there you're getting the cream of the crop. I've always thought that in general teaching fellows are a cut above with respect to education and intelligence. It was a great way of getting people into the teaching profession when we had a serious deficit."

Visit Vault at **www.vault.com** for insider company profiles, expert advice, career message boards, expert resume reviews, the Vault Job Board and more.

VAULT CAREER LIBRARY

41

Disadvantages

Despite their obvious advantages, however, alternative certification programs have disadvantages, both for aspiring teachers and the schools where they are placed. For starters, on the one hand, the teaching shortage problem in the United States has become much less severe in recent years, due in large part to the growing number of alternative certification programs. Now, teacher vacancies, if not filled by fully certified teachers, are frequently filled by people in the process of obtaining their certification. But alternative certification programs have high teacher dropout rates, in part because they take people with little or no teaching experience and place them in teaching situations that would be difficult for many experienced teachers.

To wit, despite the fact that teachers enter these programs after agreeing to teach in a high-needs school for several years, a significant percentage of teachers in these programs drop out before completing the program. And many others leave the field of education within several years of completing their obligations. Steve Tullin cites this as one of the major disadvantages to these types of programs. He believes that many people "use the program as a vehicle to gain a free master's. After completing the program they often flee the system or to go into other jobs, sometimes the same jobs they came from in the beginning. The very nature of the fellows is that they're willing to pop in and out of professions. If they feel wanderlust they'll get up and go. Traditionally trained educators are more likely to stay in the field."

It's important to note, however, that although many members of alternative certification programs do eventually leave the field, many others do continue teaching. Sam Jordan, a graduate of Teach for America who now is an assistant law professor at Washington University, says, "I tend to be in favor of the alternative certification program. I know a lot of people from Teach for America who are still teaching. One of my best friends is now a principal in the Chicago schools."

Understanding attrition

As stated above, the high dropout rate may be due in large part to the fact that these programs place people in extremely difficult teaching situations before they've gone through the conventional training and certification process—an experience that makes many people feel frustrated and overwhelmed. Of course, it is also difficult to teach full time and attend master's degree courses at the same time. However, some alternative certification participants, such as Sam Jordan, feel that completing teacher training while working in the classroom makes it more meaningful. "The disadvantage of the master's route [to certification] is that teaching is something that's hard to talk about without having done it. Alternative certification programs are extremely relevant because you're trying to succeed and survive in the classroom. Training is more hypothetical before you're actually in the classroom."

The experiences of people who join alternative certification programs may also be determined by the climates of the schools in which they are placed. The degree to which these teachers feel supported by the administration and their colleagues may radically affect the way they feel about their teaching positions. Sam Jordan says, "One huge issue with alternative certification programs is that sometimes existing teachers aren't willing to accept teachers from those backgrounds, and when this happens it can be extremely isolating. I had a lot of friends who struggled with that, although I wasn't one of those people. Parents can also sometimes be suspicious of young, privileged teachers coming into building. However, I only experienced this in a couple isolated incidents. But other schools had more racial tensions; they were split along racial lines. My experience was about as good as you can get from a program like Teach for America, where by definition you're going to be placed in a struggling school."

In retrospect

Those who graduate from alternative certification programs—whether or not they decide to remain in the field—almost always feel it is a challenging experience. Debbie Beaudin says of the New York City Teaching Fellows, "It's really hard. It's hard to take classes while you're teaching full time. It's hard to go into the classroom without having that much experience, which the program forces you to do." At the same time, she says, "I would do it the same way if I had to do it over again."

Chad Hamilton has mixed feelings about his experience in an alternative certification program, although he decided to continue teaching after fulfilling his two-year obligation to the Teaching Fellows. "I don't feel that the Teaching Fellows prepares people in any way whatsoever for the actual job of teaching. They're relatively effective at recruiting people and strategically informing them about what's in store for them. A lot of people join without having a sense of the work it takes to teach full time and go to graduate school. It's good in the sense that if you want to teach and are changing careers, or if this is your first job and you don't have an education degree, it can be a good opportunity—if you're the right person. Most Teaching Fellows are sent to the most difficult schools in New York, and if you can be successful in a difficult New York City school while meeting the demands of a master's program, that leaves you pretty well equipped to teach anywhere in United States."

James De Francesco, an assistant principal who was once a Teaching Fellow says that while he thinks that many people in alternative teacher certification programs do not receive adequate support, "in theory I think they are absolutely fantastic for number of reasons. It's smart use of resources, a great way to bring second-career people with maturity and a certain skill set into the classroom, and a great way to get dedicated people into high-needs subjects and high needs schools. It's a great way of getting people into the classroom who truly want to be there."

A challenging start

Certainly, alternative certification programs are not the best path for every aspiring teacher. People who enter such programs should expect their experience—particularly during the first year—to be demanding and exhausting. They should also be aware that, although there are a number of significant advantages to these programs, many people believe that these programs expect too much of new teachers. Clara Lin, a New York City elementary school teacher who became certified through a master's with certification program, says that she is "skeptical of fast-track, alternative certification programs. They take people who are very interested in becoming educators and put them through extreme duress. I don't think its fair to the students or teachers. However, they are good opportunities for people who don't have money or don't want to take out loans for graduate education. I think that we need other, cheaper opportunities to train teachers and give them better support so that teachers are not forced to enter programs that will burn them out before they have the chance to learn."

Teaching in a "High-Needs" School

Everyone who considers enrolling in an alternative certification program is aware that these programs place teachers in high-needs schools. However, many people do not know exactly what to expect in such an environment, particularly with regard to student behavior and disciplinary problems. To some extent, Hollywood and the media have perpetuated terrifying images of inner-city schools in the public imagination. As a result, many people fear that teaching at a high-needs school will mean putting themselves in the way of physical harm on a daily basis. In reality, this is an exaggerated depiction.

The truth is that high-needs schools are often identified as such because of low standardized test scores. Some of them have very few discipline problems, while others have serious discipline problems. It is wise for teachers entering an alternative certification program to be as involved in their school placement as the program allows—and, if possible, to visit their prospective school before committing to the program. While some alternative certification programs give teachers no input as to where they are placed, other programs, such as the New York City Teaching Fellows, have placement fairs where teachers can speak with principals and interview for specific school placements. This opportunity to meet and speak with school administrators, ask questions, and get a feel for what a school is really like can be invaluable.

Perspectives on unruly behavior

Some schools that participate in alternative certification programs do have serious discipline problems, which may in some cases lead to student violence. However, the prospective teacher who is thinking of joining an alternative certification program should be aware that this violence is almost always between students; teachers rarely face physical threats from their students. At the same time, the worry of coming across a student fight in the hallway—or worse yet, in one's own classroom—can become a real source of stress for a teacher.

Debbie Beaudin says that although classroom disruptions are a problem in the high school she joined as a New York City Teaching Fellow, there is virtually no crime or violence in the school. "My school is not very fight-heavy. The main things that happen are talking in classroom and small disruptions. Students like to play-fight, and there's a lot of immaturity. But they're not aggressive. They're never aggressive to me. Well, once in a while maybe a little verbal aggression, as in 'why are you making me work so hard?' The main problem is that they often see teachers as adversaries rather than team members."

Visit Vault at www.vault.com for insider company profiles, expert advice, career message boards, expert resume reviews, the Vault Job Board and more.

VAULT CAREER LIBRARY

45

Sam Jordan, who taught fourth grade in Washington D.C. through Teach for America, describes the student behavior in his school as average. "On the whole, our school was better than other schools in terms of behavior, because the teachers had all adopted a similar approach to discipline at some basic level. There was an agreed-upon way that students should act. My experience wasn't really harrowing in terms of behavior; I just encountered classroom disruptions and some frustrating challenges to authority. But I didn't have huge problems with student behavior," he said.

Special needs

Chad Hamilton joined the New York City Teaching Fellows and asked for a placement with special needs, emotionally disturbed children. This is a potentially chaotic environment, but like the others quoted in this section, Chad finds that most of the behavior problems he encounters are relatively minor. "The things I deal with on a regular basis are keeping students attentive and on task, kids wanting to get out of their seats or talk to the others next to them about a completely unrelated topic. They have problems sitting still, and they have difficulty staying seated. Once or twice a day we get to the point where I have to directly confront a student's behavior. Usually I can do it with humor, or by giving the student a reason to get out of his seat for a few minutes. They're so easily distracted that it's pretty easy. I don't have to deal with flying desks and chairs and fist fights. It's different for every kid. One I might be able to disarm with humor, and another I might have to yell at because that's the only thing he'll respond to. I have a very supportive atmosphere in my classroom where we're always being positive and supportive to each other."

Things to remember

Although teachers going into a high-needs school have reasons to be especially concerned about behavior problems, the reality is that any new teacher, particularly one who has little experience working with children, will find the first year of teaching to be stressful. Furthermore, it's worth noting that student behavior can be a problem in any school— it is not a problem that is exclusive to schools with low test scores.

In all likelihood, most challenges new teachers face in high-needs schools will come from immaturity, and a lack of interest in academic activities, rather than out-and-out aggression. However, when faced with this type of constant disruption—no matter how silly—teachers sometimes feel frustrated and ineffectual.

And even when students behave themselves, it may be frustrating to try to motivate and educate them. When many students in a classroom have serious academic deficits, a teacher will frequently feel as if there is simply not enough time to give all the students the attention that they need to improve their skills. As a result, many people who teach students in low-performing schools constantly worry that they are not doing enough for their students.

Paying your dues

James De Francesco says that while his initial placement as a New York City Teaching Fellow was particularly difficult, he believes that this experience fueled his passion for the field of education. "If my first job out of college as a twenty-one-year-old graduate was to step inside a school with the type of insanity as the one where I first taught, I wouldn't have lasted until 3:00 p.m.. The stresses you face and the things you have to cope with in 20 minutes are more than what a chiropractic neurosurgeon deals with," according to De Francesco. "But looking back at what it was like for me at 41 years old, I was able to take it in stride. It made two major impressions on me. The first is that there are children out there who need to be helped, no matter what their situations are. The other thing is that we hear so much about what schools like that are like, but you can't appreciate it unless you are there. You can hear about a school with desks flying out windows— but unless you're there you can't understand why it's happening. Ultimately, I think that working in that school helped me define what I wanted to do in the classroom. If I had been placed in a different type of school I don't think my passion, dedication and level of interest would be as strong."

Visit Vault at **www.vault.com** for insider company profiles, expert advice, career message boards, expert resume reviews, the Vault Job Board and more.

VAULT CAREER LIBRARY

47

Finding the Right Fit

CHAPTER 7

Qualities Employers Look For

While some schools have severe teaching shortages, others have hundreds of applications for every position. Schools in wealthy suburban areas tend to be the most competitive places to get a teaching position, and low-income areas tend to be the places with teaching shortages. However, there are many exceptional schools in low-income areas that have as many applicants for teaching positions as schools in wealthier communities.

Before applying for jobs, teachers should identify the type of school that they want to work in. Different schools have different educational philosophies, and teachers are more likely to do well in job interviews—and to find teaching positions they are happy with—if they apply to schools that are managed in a way that is consistent with their own educational philosophies. For example, a progressive school where students call teachers by their first names and learn through hands-on activities may seek different types of teachers than a school that uses a traditional curriculum that stresses reading, writing and arithmetic.

Clara Lin, who teaches in a progressive elementary school, says, "Prospective teachers looking for schools should think about schools they've had experiences in and identify the appealing and unappealing aspects of those schools. This can help them create a short list of schools where they'd like to work. If the teacher doesn't have a lot of experience, I'd recommend visiting a lot of schools. You can do some networking and see if you can do some observations or classroom visits at the schools in your area."

Once prospective teachers have identified the type they would like to teach, there are a number of qualities that they can expect potential employers to be on the lookout for, regardless of whether the school is rich or poor, progressive or traditional.

An understanding of children

School administrators want to populate their schools with teachers who not only genuinely like children but who have a solid understanding of child psychology. This knowledge may be gained in part through the educational psychology courses that are a standard part of teacher training programs— but to a large extent it comes from experience working with children.

Steve Tullin, who has served on many teacher hiring committees, feels that this is one of the most important qualities in a teacher. "They desperately need to enjoy and like children. They need to have a knowledge of adolescent psychology or a desire to learn about it. Some people go into teaching and they think that they'll be teaching a subject. In K-12 education you're not teaching a subject so much as you're teaching a class. It's not so much a matter of liking a subject; it's a matter of liking people. Sometimes teachers who are too focused on their academic subject don't realize that they're dealing with lives and special people. Teaching really is as much about psychology as it is about education."

Rachel Wadle says that in addition to "patience and flexibility," in order to be a successful teacher "you need to be easy-going, caring, and able to talk to young children."

In addition to enjoying children, successful teachers tend to have highly developed social skills and enjoy being around people in general. Administrators seek teachers who will get along with everyone and who will contribute to efforts to improve the quality of the school. They avoid teachers who they fear will cause divisiveness, and seek those who they believe will be cooperative.

Educational background and professional experience

Competitive school districts often give preference to job candidates who already have several years of classroom experience—in addition to advanced degrees in education or a field related to their subject area. However, most school districts do hire some teachers straight out of teacher training programs. When interviewing teachers with little experience, administrators may expect job candidates to demonstrate their knowledge of teaching through a portfolio that contains sample lessons. Teachers also may be asked to present a lesson to the school hiring committee.

Although teachers with classroom experience may have an edge in the hiring process, in some cases school districts seek out new teachers because they can be hired in at the bottom of the teacher salary scale. Although the practice of exclusively hiring new teachers and overlooking those with experience to save money is frowned upon by teachers' unions, this continues to be a reality in the world of education.

Prospective teachers should also be aware that written responses to the essay portions of job applications are viewed as a reflection of their intellectual capabilities and educational backgrounds. Brigid Tileston, who is on the hiring committee of a school that typically receives 3,000 applications for every teaching position, says "we look for good writing on the essay portions of applications. We've sometimes not given interviews based on writing."

Organizational skills

The successful classroom teacher must be able to juggle many tasks, including planning daily lessons, grading papers, communicating with parents, decorating the classroom and filling out paperwork. This is all in addition to the time actually spent teaching students. This need to wear many hats is something that many teachers find challenging, if not overwhelming— and a teacher who falls behind may find it difficult to catch up.

Furthermore, organization and consistency in the classroom are important tools for maintaining student performance and behavior. For example, if teachers fail to return student assignments in a timely manner, students will lose their motivation to complete tasks to the best of their ability. Or if teachers tell students that they are going to call their parents and then don't, pupils begin to see the teachers' promises as hollow. Therefore, school hiring committees usually look for people who demonstrate an ability to juggle multiple tasks. And at an interview you should expect to be asked questions about how you handle tasks such as lesson planning and grading.

Creativity

Even teachers who work in schools with scripted curricula must be able to design course units and plan lessons with creativity. Students will become bored if asked to do the same types of worksheets and activities every day. Therefore, a successful teacher will present students with different types of lessons and activities that are tailored to the material being studied—and will constantly evaluate their teaching methods and look for new ways to present information to students. This is why many employers ask teachers to present sample lesson plans as a part of the interview process.

James De Francesco, who currently works as an assistant principal, says that when he hires teachers, the ability to convey information with creativity is extremely important. "I look for someone who makes a lesson engaging and accessible—and someone who is willing to deal with disparate levels of ability in the classroom. I don't want someone who will just sit at the desk and say 'your work is on the board,' but I also don't want someone who will bring in a guitar and sing Kumbaya. I'm looking for someone who treats students fairly and equitably and who knows their stuff.

Visit Vault at **www.vault.com** for insider company profiles, expert advice, career message boards, expert resume reviews, the Vault Job Board and more.

VAULT CAREER LIBRARY

51

I want to see lessons that will make students want to come back to your class tomorrow."

Casie Smith, who mentors preschool teachers, says that when she interviews teachers she also looks for innovative teaching techniques. "I think that what makes a great early educator is someone who possesses all of the things that we try to impart on the children: curiosity, a love for learning, creativity. Creativity is very important."

Classroom presence

To a certain extent, teachers are performers, and they are expected to be engaging and entertaining in the classroom. While some teachers conduct lessons in a theatrical manner, other teachers deliver information in a more straightforward way. Either of these approaches is appropriate, so long as the teachers can successfully keep students on-task and engaged in relevant learning activities.

Steve Tullin says classroom presence "is like the *it factor* Hollywood talks about. Some people have it, some don't. In my position I learned how to size people up so that I could tell who was going to be good, who was going to need to work at it, and who might not make it no matter how hard they tried."

The need for an engaging classroom presence is especially important in schools where students are often behind grade level and academically unmotivated. In schools where students are well-behaved, teachers often do not need to work as hard to develop this dynamism in order to ensure student success, but this does not mean that classroom presence isn't important in this type of environment. "I've seen some very mediocre teaching in schools where the kids are very well behaved," Tullin says.

Willingness to participate in extracurricular activities

Most schools, especially at the secondary level, have extracurricular programs. In most cases, these activities are organized and led by school faculty members. The willingness of teachers to get involved with these activities is viewed as an asset by many schools, and something that many administrators look for when hiring teachers. In return, many teachers— particularly those just starting out—welcome this opportunity to earn the extra money in exchange for leading school activities.

Competitive school districts often have extensive extracurricular activities for students, and as a result, they truly need teachers who are willing to lead drama clubs, chess clubs, sports teams and the like. In some school districts, participation in extracurricular activities may be a condition of employment. This is something that many teachers are happy to do, both because of the financial compensation and because it is something they truly enjoy. However, other teachers find that this type of involvement eats into their free time more than they would like, because the teaching profession is demanding enough on its own. Therefore, before applying for a teaching position, it's important to decide how you feel about devoting time to extracurricular activities. No job applicant should commit to leading an extracurricular activity simply to get a job. It is dishonest to make a promise you do not intend to fulfill, and teachers who lead activities halfheartedly do a disservice to the students who participate in them.

Brigid Tileston says that her desire to direct high school theater is the primary reason why she was able to get a teaching job in a school district where there are typically thousands of applicants for every English teaching position. And as a member of her school's hiring committee, she now finds herself looking for candidates with the interest and ability to lead extra-curricular groups. "On our website, you can search applicants based on their ability to lead extracurricular activities, and with the amount of extra-curricular activities that our school offers we're looking for what teachers can do inside and outside classroom."

However, Brigid believes that though extracurricular activities can help you get your foot in the door, this is only one quality that administrators look for. "My experience with theater got me my job. But I should stress that, while being a theater person got me noticed, they wouldn't have hired me if I were sub-par in the interview. But being interested in extracurricular activities is a way to get you noticed."

Finding a School That is Right For You

Although every new teacher is, understandably, eager to find a job, it's important for candidates to identify schools that have an educational philosophy and environment that is a good fit with their own personalities and goals.

The spectrum of schools where you might apply for a job is, of course, dictated to a certain extent by your geographical area of the country. Teachers in large, urban areas will have many schools to choose from, while teachers in smaller communities have fewer. However, even in a small community, the working environments in different schools may vary significantly. All new teachers should think carefully about the school or

Visit Vault at **www.vault.com** for insider company profiles, expert advice, career message boards, expert resume reviews, the Vault Job Board and more.

VAULT CAREER LIBRARY

53

schools in their area where they would most like to work. And once you've created a list of schools where you would like to work, you should use your networking skills to speak with teachers and administrators in the schools where you plan to apply for work.

Creating a shortlist

In a traditional training program, teachers-in-training typically have the opportunity to visit many different types of schools. After graduating, they should use these experiences as guidelines when creating a list of places where they plan to apply for jobs. As stated earlier, new teachers should think about the schools they've had experiences in and identify the appealing and unappealing aspects of both, using this to create a short list of schools where they think they'd like to teach. If a teacher doesn't have a lot of experience, visiting schools and networking are essential.

Sounding out staff

New teachers should also speak with faculty members in the types of schools where they want to work. Chad Hamilton says, "If you're looking to teach, and you're looking for some insight, you should talk to someone in the situation you anticipate being in. If you're going to do 8 to 1 to 1 special education, talk to teachers in that situation. If you're going to teach in an urban school, teachers in public, city classrooms can offer you the most relevant information."

James De Francesco says someone seeking a job should always "take a look at the climate or culture of the school, and think about how it affects the children in the school. The staff of a good school will have a unified vision, and a shared responsibility—there will be a feeling that everyone is rolling in the same direction." Also, with the current emphasis on standardized testing, it's important for a teacher to look at "what a school does for its students—what programs it has for them. Is it preparing kids to be good test takers or good problem solvers? The goal of a school should be to develop thinkers and researchers."

School websites

Beyond your own experiences in different types of classrooms, look at school report cards to identify the schools where you'd most like to work. Websites such as insideschools.org give teachers an opportunity to see reviews of specific schools by teachers, parents and city authorities. This little bit of research can go a long way in helping you secure a position that will meet your expectations.

Chase your choices

Once you've narrowed down the field, be assertive in pursuing the schools you're interested in. Job seekers should contact administrators at all of the schools where they would like to work, says Clara Lin. "A lot of schools don't post vacancies," she says, "although in some areas they are required to do so legally. But I'd recommend sending resumes to the schools you're interested in, whether or not you think that they have a vacancy."

Clara's proactive approach to the job search helped her find a position in the exact type of school where she wanted to work. Upon finishing her degree, Clara visited a number of websites dedicated to progressive education; an e-mail to one of these sites resulted in a contact that referred her to the school where she teaches today.

After conducting a job search in an area with a very competitive job market for teachers, Jim Tileston also learned that an aggressive approach can pay off. "Lots of school districts will say on their websites, 'do not contact us directly.' But even in these districts, contacting department chairs directly is absolutely essential. I don't know anyone who's been hired who did not do this."

And be ready

It's crucial to be prepared for interest from a potential employer. "Have all of your information—your teaching license, your portfolio—in an electronic format and ready to go in case someone e-mails you and asks you for information about your background," says Jim. "This way they can look at your information immediately. In a competitive job market timing is of the essence. If they have to wait for three days for you to scan your documents, someone else may get the job."

Visit Vault at **www.vault.com** for insider company profiles, expert advice, career message boards, expert resume reviews, the Vault Job Board and more.

VAULT CAREER LIBRARY   **55**

Writing a Cover Letter and Resume

CHAPTER 8

Resumes

Education resumes follow many of the conventions used for resumes in other fields. Your resume should include both education and experience, with entries listed in reverse chronological order.

Experience

If you have prior experience in teaching or another field you should put your professional experiences first. Descriptions of prior jobs should include all relevant tasks and responsibilities. Be sure to include any involvement with extracurricular activities, on school committees, or with professional organizations.

If you have not yet worked as a classroom teacher, you should also include education-related experiences such as student teaching, working as a camp counselor or volunteering at a school. These types of experiences establish a long-standing interest in working with children, something that will make an impression on potential employers.

Education

If you have little professional experience, you may want to put your educational background at the beginning of your resume. Include any awards or academic honors you earned in college; if your grade point was over 3.0 this should also be included. You should also list all areas of academic concentration, including those unrelated to education or the subject in which you teach. The high school English teacher who did a minor in chemistry establishes him or herself as someone with well-rounded academic interests—something that is highly valued in the field of education.

Visit Vault at **www.vault.com** for insider company profiles, expert advice, career message boards, expert resume reviews, the Vault Job Board and more.

VAULT CAREER LIBRARY   **57**

Certification

An education resume should also include information about your teacher certification. In many states there are multiple types of teacher certificates, and you should list the specific type that you possess—for example, "New York State Elementary Certificate (provisional)."

Other considerations

In addition to the information described above, all resumes should contain the applicant's name and contact information, including address, phone number and e-mail. Your name should be placed near the top of the resume and printed in a larger and/or darker typeface than the words that follow.

Conventional wisdom often states that a resume should be no longer than one page. While it is important that a resume be concise, there is nothing wrong with extending a resume to two pages, but only if you have extensive relevant experience. And you should never extend a resume to three pages.

On the following pages you will find two sample resumes and cover letters, one for a new teacher who has just completed an undergraduate training program, and one for a teacher with several years of experience. The two resumes follow slightly different formats, but both are designed in a way that clearly highlights the teacher's experience and strengths in the classroom.

Sample Novice Resume

BRYAN ABRAHMAS

423 Parkside Avenue,
Chicago, IL 60601
(555) 342-3432
b.abrahams@gmail.com

EDUCATION

COLLEGE OF THE CITY OF CHICAGO   Projected Completion

Bachelor of Science in Education with focus in early education, mathematics minor.   June 2008

EDUCATION FIELDWORK

Burnside Elementary School

Student teaching   January 2008 to March 2008

Fifth grade:

- Developed mathematics, language arts, social studies and science lessons.
- Conducted a unit on fractions that allowed students to experience mathematic concepts through real-world experiences.
- Volunteered to lead an after-school music program.
- Organized a school-wide field trip to a nature center where students had the opportunity to learn about wild animals in our area.

Montgomery Academy for the Arts

Student teaching   March 2007 to June 2007

First grade:

- Developed lessons in music, science and mathematics.
- Taught a unit on nutrition and organized a school-wide "good eating" campaign.
- Created an interdisciplinary math/science unit that emphasized the ways that numbers appear in nature.

Hanover Elementary   September 2007 to December 2007

- Completed 20 observation hours in second- and third-grade classrooms.
- Helped organize school-wide math activities in celebration of "Pi Day."

Rocks and Streams Day Camp   Summer 2007

- Worked as a lead counselor at a summer nature camp for students in grades two through six.
- Organized daily nature hikes, worked with other counselors to plan nature-related art projects.

EDUCATION FIELDWORK

- Early childhood certification: grades K-3
- Mathematics certification: grades K-6

Sample Novice Cover Letter

Bryan Abrahams
423 Parkside Avenue,
Chicago, IL 60601
(555) 342-3432
b.abrahams@gmail.com

Jacob Johnson
Principal
Martin Luther King Elementary School
16 Hillbrook Lane
Chicago, Illinois 23423

June 20, 2008

Dear Mr. Johnson:

It recently came to my attention that Martin Luther King Elementary is looking for an early education instructor. Upon learning of this, I immediately completed the online application process. However, because of my high level of regard for your school, I am writing to reiterate my sincere interest in this position, and tell you a little more about myself.

Throughout my collegiate career I had the opportunity to do fieldwork in a number of remarkable schools throughout Chicago. At each of these schools, I became a contributing member of the school community by volunteering my time and energy to provide enrichment for students at the school. In addition to observing and conducting lessons, I organized a school-wide field trip, helped organize a nutrition program and volunteered in an after-school music program. As a teacher, I want to go above and beyond the call of duty, to provide valuable learning experiences to students at the school where I work, and I believe that my dedication, energy and enthusiasm would allow me to become a successful member of the MLK community.

I possess teacher certification in both math and early childhood education. As you are aware, this is an unusual combination of qualifications, and it is my goal to make math instruction enjoyable and accessible to young children.

I enclose my resume for your attention, and would like to thank you in advance for your time. If you should require any further information, or if you would like me to send you a copy of my teaching portfolio, please do not hesitate to contact me.

I look forward to speaking with you.

Yours sincerely,

Bryan Abrahams

Sample Experienced Resume

ANGELA WILKINSON

2344 West Anderson Road
Sunnyhill, California 23432
(555.234.3432)
wilkinson@yahoo.com

OBJECTIVE

To obtain a leadership position within a high school English Department.

EDUCATION

TRI–VALLEY STATE UNIVERSITY   Fox Valley, California

Master's Degree in Educational Administration   2000 to 2002

ST. MARTIN'S UNIVERSITY   St. Martin, Maryland

Bachelor of Arts with a dual major in education and English, and a minor in the performing arts.

PROFESSIONAL EXPERIENCE

Maplewood High School   Ridgefield, California

English Teacher   2002 to present

Teach American literature, British literature and speech to students in grades nine through 11.

- Coach the high school debate team.
- Serve on the school budget and English department curriculum mapping committees.
- Participate in an interdisciplinary English/history initiative.
- Represent the school English department at a one-week summer seminar dedicated to the integrative model of curriculum development.

Jefferson High School   Parkside Heights, Maryland

English Teacher   1997 to 2002

Taught English composition, creative writing and world literature to ninth grade students.

- Led the school drama club for three years.
- Participated in a program sponsored by the Parkside arts museum, which integrates art education into literacy instruction.
- Helped organize and supervise the student council's annual fundraising drive.

CALIFORNIA STATE CERTIFICATIONS

- Secondary English (grades seven to 12)
- General Administration

Visit Vault at www.vault.com for insider company profiles, expert advice, career message boards, expert resume reviews, the Vault Job Board and more.

VAULT CAREER LIBRARY

61

Sample Experienced Cover Letter

Angela Wilkinson
2344 West Anderson Road
Fox Valley, California 23432
(555.234.3432)
wilkinson@yahoo.com

Maryann Allen
Principal, Anderson High School
Fox Valley, California 23432

March 23, 2008

Dear Ms. Allen,

I recently had the opportunity to meet several members of your staff at the annual Fox Valley School Leaders convention. While working to develop curriculum initiatives for the Fox Valley School District in the coming years, Matt DeGeorge, your science department chair, suggested that I apply for the English department chair position that will be open at Anderson High School this coming fall.

Several years ago, I completed my master's in educational administration, and since that time I have become increasingly involved in the curriculum initiatives for the English department at Maplewood H.S. I believe that my educational background in school administration combined with my professional experience in content development makes me a qualified applicant for this position. My involvement with extracurricular activities, academic plans and school budgets has given me the necessary experience to implement a large-scale academic program at a large high school—and I would eagerly bring this experience to the position of English department head at Anderson High School.

Thank you for taking the time to review my qualifications. I hope that they will be of interest, and look forward to speaking with you in the near future.

Yours truly,

Angela Wilkinson

The Teaching Portfolio

Most teacher certification programs require aspiring teachers to compile a teaching portfolio as part of their training. This portfolio normally includes sample lesson and unit plans, as well as examples of exemplary student work—normally work that is acquired during student teaching. Other documents may be included in the teaching portfolio as well, including: resume, one-page statement of teaching philosophy, teacher certification exam scores, and evidence of academic achievements (transcripts, awards certificates, etc.).

A portfolio is of particular use to a new teacher with little on-the-job experience, as it gives the applicant a chance to demonstrate his or her achievements to the hiring committee. Today, the compilation of a teaching portfolio is a graduation requirement for most teacher training programs. However, even after you get your first job, you should not consider your portfolio to be a finished project. You should continually put examples of your best work—your best lessons and student work—into your portfolio. This way, if you find yourself looking for another job you will have an up-to-date and impressive body of work to show off at interviews. While the importance of a strong portfolio is greater for someone seeking a first job than for a seasoned teacher, an interview committee will be interested in seeing anything that you present to them—and if your portfolio is impressive it can help you secure a job.

Visit Vault at **www.vault.com** for insider company profiles, expert advice, career message boards, expert resume reviews, the Vault Job Board and more.

V/\ULT CAREER LIBRARY

63

The Interview

Depending on the size of the school district to which you are applying, your initial interview may be with an administrator from a specific school, or with a personnel director for an entire district. In either case, your strategy in preparing for the interview will be similar; although an interview in a personnel office is likely to be a shorter screening interview.

The following pages will discuss the ways you can prepare for a teaching interview as well as some of the topics that are covered in a typical interview for an educational position.

Preparing for the Interview

There are a number of things you can do before an interview to ensure that you make a good impression.

Dress appropriately.

You should wear a neat suit, or a jacket with matching skirt or slacks. Although certain fields have adopted casual dress codes in recent years—and although many teachers dress casually while on the job—you will be expected to look professional at an interview for a teaching position.

Bring your portfolio to the interview.

If you have a portfolio with sample curricula, lesson plans, and examples of student achievement, bring this to the interview. It is also a good idea to bring several copies of your resume to the interview.

Learn about the district or school you are interviewing with.

Schools have a wide range of educational philosophies, and curricula, and before going to an interview you should familiarize yourself with the school's educational model. Knowledge of this will help you convey interest in the position and help you anticipate the types of questions that you may be asked.

Visit Vault at **www.vault.com** for insider company profiles, expert advice, career message boards, expert resume reviews, the Vault Job Board and more.

VAULT CAREER LIBRARY

65

A great deal of information about specific schools is available online. Most schools now have websites, and there are several other sites (listed in the appendix) that gather information about schools across the country. To learn about a given school, you might also talk with teachers or parents from this school.

Questions You Will Be Asked

The questions you at the interview are likely to be posed as scenarios, or case studies, and if a question is delivered this way, you should include anecdotes from your own personal experiences in your response, letting the interviewer know that you have dealt with similar situations in your own teaching or student teaching experiences.

The following are some the questions you may be asked.

What is your philosophy on classroom management?

School administrators want to know that you will be able to keep your classroom under control. Philosophies regarding classroom management also vary widely, and the interviewer will also be interested in whether your particular philosophy of discipline is compatible with the school's. For example, if you're interviewing for a position in a school that places a great deal of importance on positive reinforcement, the interviewer will be looking for evidence that this is at the heart of your classroom management techniques.

When talking about classroom management, be honest about the way that you plan to deal with behavioral problems. Also make sure to have a disciplinary plan that consists of several different steps. This way, if the interviewer asks, "If that doesn't work, what will you do?" you'll have a ready answer.

It's also important that your classroom management plan include preventative strategies. For example, you may want to stress the way that your organizational systems reinforce order in the classroom. Interviewers will look for evidence that you see classroom management as something that extends beyond discipline.

How do you plan to communicate with parents?

When answering this question, be sure to address the variety of different circumstances under which you may communicate with parents. These may include sending out student progress reports, calling parents of students who are having academic and/or behavioral problems, and dealing with complaints from parents. Be sure to let the hiring committee know that you are willing to work with parents—even parents who are unresponsive or difficult—in a positive, constructive way.

Describe a lesson or unit of which you are particularly proud.

Be prepared to speak about one or more units that you have created. The interviewer will be looking for creative ideas that successfully fulfill a learning objective and maintain sufficient academic rigor.

If you are interviewing at a school that adheres to a particular educational philosophy, be sure to familiarize yourself with this philosophy before your interview so that you can emphasize the aspects of your lessons that are in line with those of this particular school.

Teachers interviewing for a first job will be expected to discuss lessons they created during student teaching, or as a part of their teacher education programs.

How will you integrate computers and other technology into your lessons?

Schools across the country have recognized the importance of technology in education, and they expect teachers to take advantage of whatever computer resources the school has to offer by integrating those into their lessons in exciting, creative ways. At the same time, computer resources in many schools are limited, and interviewees may be asked to describe their strategies for using limited resources to maximum advantage.

How do you address the needs of students with different learning styles and abilities?

The importance of differentiated instruction is a hot topic in education; it is also something that many teachers find difficult. Therefore, principals actively seek out teaching candidates who are able to support struggling students while at the same time challenging students who are performing at an advanced level.

Visit Vault at www.vault.com for insider company profiles, expert advice, career message boards, expert resume reviews, the Vault Job Board and more.

VAULT CAREER LIBRARY

67

How do you assess your students' understanding of a given concept?

The way you reflect upon your success in the classroom is critical. An interviewer wants reassurance that you are able to tell whether or not your students "get" a given concept. Therefore, you should be prepared to describe the evidence of understanding that you look for in your students, as well as how you use student performance on tests and projects as a way of assessing your own progress as a teacher.

What strategies do you use to motivate and engage your students?

Interviewers want evidence that you will make it a priority to inspire and motivate your students by tapping into their interests and giving them opportunities to feel successful and valued in your classroom.

How do you keep your paperwork organized?

Be prepared to outline a system for keeping track of grades, anecdotal records and other paperwork in detail. Few teachers enjoy the amount of paperwork they are responsible for, but it is an important part of the job description and the interviewer will want to know that you can stay on top of it.

Are you willing to lead any extracurricular activities?

If you are interested in leading an extracurricular activity, state this, and describe any reasons why you might be especially qualified to lead a particular activity. For example, if you played college football, you might offer to coach the school football team. Or if you minored in theater, you might offer to lead the drama club. As previously stated, the willingness to lead an extracurricular group can help you secure a job in a competitive district.

Why did you choose to specialize in your given content area?

Secondary principals want their teachers to be experts in their given subject areas. Therefore, you should be prepared to highlight any awards or achievements related to your content area, as well as make sure that you convey sincere enthusiasm for your subject area.

If you teach elementary school, you are likely to be asked why you enjoy working with young children. Or you may be asked about academic concepts such as literacy education. You will be expected to demonstrate expertise in these areas.

What strategies do you use to help students understand your content area?

You should be prepared to discuss the specific strategies that apply to your content area. If you teach elementary school, be prepared to describe the ways you use different strategies to teach different subjects. This question will be of particular importance if you teach a subject such as mathematics, which many students find difficult to connect to.

Why are you interested in teaching at our school?

Clearly, interviewers are seeking applicants who are enthusiastic about accepting a position at their school, and you should be prepared to convey sincere enthusiasm for this particular school or teaching position.

Questions You Should Ask

At the end of the interview, you will probably be given the opportunity to ask questions—and you should take advantage of this opportunity to demonstrate your intelligence and your enthusiasm for the position.

While some questions may occur to you during the interview, and you should feel free to ask them, it's also a good idea to have a few questions prepared beforehand. The following are a few sample questions you might ask.

How do teachers at your school collaborate to develop lessons and curricula?

Administrators want to compile a staff of people who are cooperative, communicative, and willing to share ideas. By asking about the school climate and how teachers in the school work together, you are demonstrating willingness to become part of the school community.

What types of professional development do you offer?

By asking about the opportunities to develop your teaching skills you show the interviewer that you want to learn new skills and see yourself as a "lifelong learner."

Visit Vault at **www.vault.com** for insider company profiles, expert advice, career message boards, expert resume reviews, the Vault Job Board and more.

V/\ULT CAREER LIBRARY   **69**

What resources (textbooks, computers, televisions, etc.) are available at your school?

The answer to this question is one that will have a big impact upon the way you teach your classes. By asking about this you show the interviewer that you are eager to incorporate whatever is available into your lessons. But if the school has few resources, be sure you do not convey your disappointment.

How involved are the parents at your school?

It's always a good idea to acknowledge the importance of parents in a child's education.

What subjects (or "preps") will I be teaching?

At the secondary level, teachers may be given several different courses to teach, each of which will require separate preparation time. (For example, a science teacher might teach biology, physics, and chemistry courses.) At the elementary school level, a teacher might teach all subject areas, or the students might travel to a separate classroom for one or more academic subject areas—such as math or art. The specific schedule you will be teaching is something you need to know before accepting a teaching position.

Interviewing for an Administrative Position

At an interview for an administrative position you can also expect to be asked about discipline, academics, and pedagogical theory, but these questions will be framed in an administrative perspective.

The most important difference between a teaching interview and an administrative interview is that at the administrative interview you will also be asked about how you plan to manage the adults in your building. The following are a few of the questions you might be asked:

What would you do if a group of teachers became a divisive influence?

This, unfortunately, is a common problem in schools, and the interviewer will want reassurance that you are able to handle a situation like this with strength and diplomacy.

How would you handle a parent complaint about a specific teacher?

Again, the hiring committee will want evidence that you can handle complaints with diplomacy. In this particular situation it is important that you show sympathy for the parent's concerns while refraining from saying anything damaging about the teacher in question—regardless of what you might privately think about this teacher's performance.

How would you support a teacher who is having trouble controlling the class?

As an administrator you are responsible for helping teachers gain the skills they need to succeed in the classroom. While in this situation you might need to intervene with the students, you also need to devise strategies for helping this teacher develop better classroom management skills.

How would you support a teacher who is not teaching the class with sufficient academic rigor?

When answering a question like this, you need to demonstrate an understanding of the different things that might cause this situation. For example, the teacher might not have sufficient understanding of the subject matter. Or maybe the teacher is an expert in the subject area but lacks the pedagogical techniques of an effective teacher. As an administrator you need to know that these two different scenarios need to be handled differently.

How would you handle a situation where a teacher routinely showed up late to work (or required disciplinary action for another reason)?

Again, you will want to show the interviewer that you are strong enough to deal with this situation firmly, but diplomatic enough address the situation with tact and consideration.

If the district made drastic changes to the core curriculum, how would you support your teachers in adjusting to this change?

School districts frequently change their curricula in an effort to improve student performance—often to the dismay of teachers who are reluctant to adjust their tried-and-true methods for delivering instruction. You should let the hiring committee know that you will expect teachers to make any required adjustments to the curricula, and that you will show sympathy for

Visit Vault at **www.vault.com** for insider company profiles, expert advice, career message boards, expert resume reviews, the Vault Job Board and more.

VAULT CAREER LIBRARY

71

their concerns and give them the tools they need to successfully implement any mandated changes.

What staff development initiatives would you like to organize as a school administrator?

As a school leader you are expected to help teachers develop their skills; and before an interview you should have several ideas in place for how to facilitate teachers' continuing education.

When hiring teachers, what qualities would you look for?

In order to lead a staff effectively, you need to be able to make good hiring decisions. This requires good judgment of character and a solid understanding of what makes a good teacher. Be prepared to speak intelligently on these topics at the job interview.

How will you evaluate the teachers in your building?

As an administrator you need to evaluate the performance of the teachers you supervise; at an interview you should be able to articulate the things you will look for when visiting classrooms and conducting formal observations.

What leadership initiatives have you undertaken in your current (or previous) positions?

Your response to this question will be particularly important if you are applying for a first administrative position. It is important that you be able to describe at least one way that you have embraced a leadership role within your current position. For example, if you organized a school fundraiser, or acted as the point person on an academic initiative, you can cite this as evidence of your leadership abilities.

What type of school community would you like to facilitate in your building?

To be a successful school leader you need to have a vision for your school. And at an interview for an administrative position you should be able to articulate this vision, and the reasons why you think your vision would create an ideal learning environment.

ON THE JOB

EDUCATION
CAREERS

Teaching at Different Grade Levels

CHAPTER 10

Within the field of education there are many different types of jobs, each of which offers its own specific challenges and rewards. In this section, we will describe many of these educational roles in detail. If you already know which area you wish to pursue, this information will give you valuable information about your chosen career. If you are still not sure what type of educational career you want to pursue, this section may help you to identify the type of educational career that will be right for you.

When pursuing a career in education, one of the first things you need to decide upon is the age level of students you want to work with. If you're pursuing a career in secondary education, you will also need to choose an academic specialty area (such as English, math, or science). Many early education teachers also focus on a specialty area within elementary education. Although this is not required, many employers view specialized training as a valuable quality in an early education teacher. For example, many elementary school teachers specialize in literacy techniques.

Narrowing down the field

For some people, deciding upon the age level and content area that they want to teach is easy. For example, these people know instinctively that they want to teach middle school English, or early childhood education. However, there are many other people who know that they want to teach, but are not sure which level would be the best fit for them. If you fall into this category, the best way to make this decision is by looking for opportunities to work with children at different age levels. Many undergraduate programs in education help teachers-in-training to make this decision by giving them the opportunity to observe students at different age levels. If you are entering a teacher-training program as a career changer, you should find opportunity to do volunteer work with children at different age levels before committing to a specific age group. For example, you might work with a community organization that does tutoring, or lead a children's activity groups through a sports club, church group or organization such as the Boy Scouts. Many of these groups are short on volunteers and will welcome your assistance. These are all opportunities to work with children while also giving something back to your communities—and most people find that they are able to quickly identify the age level that they want to teach after gaining first-hand experience with groups of children.

Preschool

In recent years, studies have shown that attendance in a preschool can greatly increase a child's social and intellectual skills, providing a solid academic foundation that will help the child succeed in elementary school. As a result, there are now more children enrolled in preschool programs than ever before. Since 1965, the Head Start Program, which is run by the United States Department of Health and Human Services, has offered free preschool education to children from low-income families. In addition to the impact of parental awareness of the benefits of preschool, the increasing availability of affordable preschool has played a large role in the large percentage of young children who are now enrolled in preschool programs.

Preschool children

During the preschool years, children experience rapid intellectual growth. Their vocabularies expand rapidly, along with their ability to use language to communicate thoughts and feelings. Children at this age are typically eager to have new experiences, and their curiosity about the world often leads to endless questions—which can sometimes be frustrating to the adults who care for them.

When children enter preschool, they are typically just beginning to show an interest in making friends and playing with other children. During these years, children's social skills develop rapidly. The preschool setting gives children the opportunity to explore their interest in socializing with other children, and to learn how to play cooperatively. However, because preschool children are just learning how to interact with others, they often need guidance on how to behave appropriately.

Preschool children frequently test authority through defiant behavior. They will often say "no" to something for the express purpose of seeing the results of their negative response. Children at this age develop a desire for freedom, and enjoy being allowed to make choices. They begin to show an interest in things that they perceive as being "adult," and enjoy being asked to help adults with chores and activities. Their sense of personal responsibility is rapidly developing, along with a sense of right and wrong behavior.

Teaching preschool

Preschool-level activities are primarily centered on play and creative activities. At this age, children's social and language capabilities change dramatically, and this development can be greatly enhanced through day-to-day interactions with other children and adults. Preschool classrooms include a generous amount of free time combined with activities such as singing, art projects and story time. Instruction in basic information—such as different colors and different types of animals—also plays a role in most preschools, but the emphasis is primarily on play and socialization.

Preschool is the only educational step during which all facets of a child's development are treated as equally important—once a child enters kindergarten, the emphasis on academics becomes much greater, and this focus becomes more intense with each school year. Casie Smith, who mentors teachers at a preschool, says, "In early education, the idea of teaching the whole child is emphasized. You're not just thinking about cognitive development, you're thinking of physical development, social development, emotional development and intellectual development. To be a great early childhood educator you need to value each of these domains, not just the cognitive."

Teachable moments

Smith says that early childhood teachers need to remember that every moment in preschool is a "teachable moment" for the children. "In the older grades, parts of the day like snack time are viewed as a necessity because the kids need to eat. In early education this is part of the curriculum, because this is when the children learn a lot of social skills. They learn how to pass materials, how to negotiate their space with others, how to feed themselves, how to experience different types of food. They learn different words to describe their food like 'mushy' and 'sweet.' Things like that are a huge part of the day."

Energy and patience required

Although preschools typically have low student-teacher ratios, it takes a lot of energy to work with very young children. It also requires extreme patience, because children this age are prone to temper tantrums and crying. Children this age are not always fully toilet trained, and a preschool teacher needs to be prepared for the occasional "accident." It takes exceptional

Visit Vault at www.vault.com for insider company profiles, expert advice, career message boards, expert resume reviews, the Vault Job Board and more.

VAULT CAREER LIBRARY

77

kindness and empathy to work with preschoolers, because children this age frequently may become upset or frustrated by ordinary daily events, and need the support of adults who will take their feelings seriously.

Qualifications

Qualifications to teach preschool vary widely. In the past, it was only necessary to have a high school diploma, but the qualifications for teaching preschool are quickly becoming more rigorous. Several years ago, a regulation was passed that requires all Head Start teachers to have an associate's degree. Additionally, many states now have regulations stating that preschool teachers must have a four-year college degree. While there is no formal certification process for preschool teachers, as there is for K-12 teachers, many preschools require teachers to have a degree in early education, developmental psychology, or another field related to the development of young children. Private preschools that follow a specific educational philosophy, such as Montessori, may also require teachers to attend a specialized teacher-training program.

Other considerations

Most preschool programs do not require students to attend school on a full-time basis. Student may come to school for half-days, or for two or three days of the week. Many preschools have different groups of students (i.e., a morning class and an afternoon class), so that the teachers work full time, but with two or more different groups of students. Other preschools may only operate on certain days of the week, or they may allow teachers to work part time, teaching with one group of students, rather than several. As a result, a career in preschool education is a good choice for someone who wants a flexible work environment or part-time employment.

For someone who enjoys working with very young children, a career as a preschool teacher can be especially rewarding because it allows you to ensure that students' first experience with school is a positive one. According to Rachel Wadle, who teaches pre-kindergarten at a public elementary school, preschool is a growing area within education. "There are state grants offered for preschool in Iowa so all kids in the district can go to preschool for free. I think the state is finally seeing that going to a quality preschool affects the rest of their education."

A preschool teacher also has the opportunity to work with children during some of their most formative years. Smith began a degree in childhood development with the goal of becoming an academic researcher in human development. Her coursework required that she do observations in daycare centers and preschools, and when she observed the enormous impact that preschool teachers have on their students, she decided that this was the right career for her. "I always feel honored to be able to experience a child's first years, and to witness these children grow in such enormous, amazing ways," she says. "At this age there's such a huge change from the beginning of the year to end of the year. Students enter the school as babies, and by the end of the year they're walking, using language, socially interacting with other children, and making connections to things in their environment. It's an honor to watch it and an honor to be a part of it."

Elementary Education

Because elementary school spans a number of years—during which children undergo dramatic developmental changes—it is often described in terms of lower-elementary school and upper-elementary school, with lower-elementary typically consisting of kindergarten through third grade and upper elementary consisting of grades four through six.

Because the characteristics of elementary school children—and the roles of an elementary school teacher—are largely dependent upon the specific grade level being taught, we will discuss the developmental characteristics of upper- and lower-elementary school students separately.

Lower-elementary school children

Students at the lower grade levels have short attention spans. As a result, an early education teacher needs to have lesson plans that include a variety of different activities that will keep students focused.

Children in early elementary school are interested in learning the difference between right and wrong. They are concerned about following rules, and frequently seek out adult approval for behavior that they believe is "correct." The preoccupation with following rules frequently leads to "tattling." However, despite their strong desire for approval, children this age will sometimes test out negative behaviors in order to see the reactions that these behaviors will provoke.

Lower-elementary school students place a great deal of importance on their friendships. They often have one "best friend," and are likely to categorize other children as either "friends" or "enemies." At this age, children usually

Visit Vault at www.vault.com for insider company profiles, expert advice, career message boards, expert resume reviews, the Vault Job Board and more.

VAULT CAREER LIBRARY   79

seek out friendships with members of the same sex, becoming more segregated by gender and showing little interest in the opposite sex.

When early elementary school students feel as if they have failed at something they often become distressed; they do not yet have the ability to critique their own work and behavior. Therefore, it is critical for the lower-elementary teacher to maintain a positive tone when giving students feedback, and to facilitate cooperative activities rather than competitive ones.

Process and results

During the early elementary school years, children develop an interest in the processes that are followed to achieve different results. In both their academic assignments and play, they typically demonstrate their interest in how to do different things, and why different processes may yield different results. Children at this age are highly imaginative and enjoy creative, artistic activities. As a result of their active imaginations they are frequently frightened by scary stories or movies.

Upper-elementary school students

At this age, children begin to develop an ability to work independently for extended stretches of time. Their desire to know why people do different things increases, and they begin to develop a more sophisticated moral viewpoint—rather than just an adherence to the rules. This viewpoint is often translated into situations being described as "fair" and "not fair." When students believe that they are being treated unfairly, they often become defiant and have a tendency to "talk back." They are beginning to see themselves as adults and feel insulted when they believe that adults do not take their thoughts or feelings seriously.

A sense of independence

Upper elementary school students have an ever-increasing sense of independence and are less solicitous of adult approval than students at the earlier grade levels. While seeking independence from adults, children this age are extremely interested in developing a social group of children their own age. They enjoy group activities, and often create their own clubs or societies. A feeling of acceptance is important to children this age, and they usually become distressed if they feel rejected by their peer group. Social groups tend to be single gender, with children showing some antagonism towards the opposite sex.

Children at this age are developing a sense of who they are as people, and frequently enjoy experimenting with different behaviors and identities. They are likely to make statements such as "I am a tomboy," or "I am popular." An interest in what "I will be when I grow up" is also common among children this age.

Upper elementary school students are developing an ability to see things from different points of view, and are capable of increased empathy for the feelings of others. They no longer see themselves as the center of the universe, but as part of a community.

Teaching elementary school

In kindergarten and the early grades, children spend a great deal of time learning how to play with other children and getting exposure to new experiences. As children progress through elementary school, academic content becomes increasingly rigorous.

Kindergarten students typically learn their letters and numbers, and are introduced to the sounds that different letters make. In first grade, children learn how to read. This is a critical step, because literacy is a precondition for all the years of education that will follow. Therefore, kindergarten and first grade teachers are likely to possess specialized training in literacy instruction. In recent years, government-sponsored programs have placed an increasing emphasis on early education, and many schools receive government grants for early literacy training. This may include intensive one-on-one literacy support for children who have difficulties learning to read.

Early intervention

Elementary school teachers are expected to identify children with academic difficulties, so that these children can receive whatever additional academic support is available in the school. (This is expected of all teachers, but this responsiblity is particularly important for teachers who work with children during their first years, because early intervention can prevent academic difficulties later on, and because many learning disabilities frequently go unnoticed until a child enters school.)

Multiple subjects

Elementary school teachers are required to teach multiple subject to their students. These usually include language arts, social studies and science. They also frequently teach math, although in many schools students travel to a different teacher for math instruction, particularly in the upper grades.

Visit Vault at www.vault.com for insider company profiles, expert advice, career message boards, expert resume reviews, the Vault Job Board and more.

VAULT CAREER LIBRARY   81

Elementary school teachers do not have the intense paper-grading responsibilities of secondary teachers, but they usually spend more time planning their lessons, something that is necessary because they are responsible for teaching multiple subjects to the same group of students. Because elementary school students—even in the higher grades—tend to have short attention spans, teachers need to have meticulously planned lessons. These lessons should include backup activities as well, in case the lesson goes more quickly than expected. This is important because students at this age need to have structured activities and "down time" in the classroom will often lead to chaos.

Middle school

In many school districts, grades five and six are housed in a middle school building. However, teachers in these grades typically possess elementary school certification (or, in some states, elementary school certification with a "middle school extension"). In this type of middle school, the instruction of fifth- and sixth-grade students usually follows the elementary school model, with one teacher delivering the majority of their instruction in multiple subject areas.

Notes from the field

Clara Lin, who teaches first grade, says that elementary school teachers need a different set of skills than secondary school teachers. "Teaching early education requires a really good understanding of childhood development; you need to know what they are going through cognitively at every age, and be able to anticipate their needs. At the junior high and high school levels it is more important to have an understanding of the challenges students may be facing, such as whether they have learning difficulties, or a history of economic or emotional hardship. When you're a teacher of younger kids, you're an expert on how children develop. When you work with older students you need to understand how the child's history will affect their learning. When you teach younger kids you're teaching them something they're learning for the first time. With older kids, you're quite possibly teaching them something they've been trying to learn for the last ten years, and this takes a quite different kind of expertise."

Because children develop so rapidly in their early years, it is common for elementary school teachers to have a "favorite grade." This was true for Betsy Sullivan, who was a classroom teacher for 17 years before becoming a school counselor. "I loved third grade," she says, "At that age, they're still innocent and eager to learn, and they have a good sense of humor. By end of year they are really ready to move on to become upper elementary students."

Chad Hamilton says that he enjoys working with elementary school students for similar reasons. "I like elementary students because I feel like they still have a sense of wonder and curiosity that some older kids just don't possess anymore. All the students in my classroom genuinely want to learn. I don't know if any of them could give you an explanation for why, but they all have an innate curiosity about the world that I find endearing. When I did summer school teaching in my first year of being a teacher I worked with seventh and eighth grade students. With some of them, the genuine desire to learn did not appear to exist—and this was something I had trouble coming to terms with. I had trouble teaching kids who claimed to not want to learn. I thought that was problematic in working with older kids. With elementary school kids that's not an issue; all of them see the real value in education."

A Day in the Life: Elementary School Teacher

Clara Lin always knew that she wanted to work in the field of education, but she wasn't sure exactly what she wanted to do, so she decided not to pursue the traditional, undergraduate path to teacher certification. After graduating from college she decided to look for a position in adult education, and soon found a position teaching English language learners at a nonprofit social services agency. In this capacity, she taught English to adult students from all over the world. Eventually, she was promoted and became the co-coordinator of a family literacy program; this gave her the opportunity to work with entire families, promoting literacy of both the parents and children.

These experiences working with families helped Clara decide to become an elementary school teacher. "I realized I was interested in taking what I'd learned from teaching adults and using it to teach children," she says.

A foot in the door

Clara believes that her decision to work in an education-related position before pursuing teacher certification was a good one. "Definitely, if someone is interested in teaching they should try to get their foot in the door by working for some sort of educational organization. Before you go to graduate school you should be sure that you really want to teach. An

Visit Vault at **www.vault.com** for insider company profiles, expert advice, career message boards, expert resume reviews, the Vault Job Board and more.

V\ULT CAREER LIBRARY

83

alarming number of teachers leave the profession after a few years, but the more experience someone has with children and teaching, the more secure they will be in their decision to become a teacher."

Once Clara was sure that she wanted to pursue a career as a classroom elementary school teacher, she enrolled in a master's with certification program. While pursuing her degree, Clara continued to work full-time as a literacy coordinator, up until her student teaching semester.

Clara's school

After graduating, Clara found a job in a progressive elementary school in New York City. The school is a part of the NYC Empowerment Zone, which means that it is not affected by some of the regulations that are imposed upon other NYC schools.

Clara's school is located in a neighborhood that has gone through a great deal of gentrification. As a result, her school is "more diverse than any other public school I've been to or seen. It's common for a public school to have a very high percentage of students from a certain racial or economic background. My school is very diverse. I have students whose parents are highly paid professionals, a student who just got out of the city shelter services, and many in between," she says.

The school where Clara works is small, which is something that she considers to be an advantage. "There's something unique about working in a school like mine. In a small school, what happens is the teachers—and not just the classroom teachers—know so many of the students so well. When families have more than one student in the school, teachers get to know the whole family. The principal knows the name and quite a bit about every student in the school. In a large school, there's no way this could happen."

Splitting grades

This year, Clara teaches a split-level first and second grade class. The philosophy behind split-grade classes is that they give students an opportunity to mentor and learn from each other. In practice, however, Clara says that it can be quite difficult to meet each child's educational needs in this type of classroom. "One of the most challenging things about teaching any grade is giving students with special needs the attention that they need—and when I say special needs I'm including students with very high ability. With a split level class it's even more challenging—you will have a first grader who's behind grade level and a second grader who's reading at a fourth grade level," she says.

While Clara has the good fortune of working in a school she loves, she also acknowledges that the first few years in the classroom are a real challenge for most teachers. She thinks the most important thing for new teachers to know is, "You are a novice teacher for three to five years. Treat those years as a time for launching your career; consider it an extension of your teacher training. Teachers should be warned against the expectation that after one year of teaching you'll know everything you need to know. Teaching is an intense career to enter, especially if you're not willing to approach it as a career where you'll be constantly improving your practice."

A day in Clara's life

5:45 a.m.:   Wake up.

6:30 a.m.:   Begin commute to work via bus and subway.

7:30 a.m.:   Arrive at work.

8:00 a.m.:   Tutor a small group of third graders in writing (as part of an extended day academic intervention program that has been implemented in all New York City schools).

8:40 a.m.:   Pick up class from the schoolyard, where they are waiting to begin their day.

8:50 a.m.:   Facilitate morning meeting with students. Students greet each other, we discuss today's schedule and go through a short community-building activity.

9:10 a.m.:   Teach word study—conduct a lesson on phonics and spelling. Afterwards, students practice phonics and spelling skills through games with a partner.

9:30 a.m.:   Teach writing workshop—conduct a 10- to 15-minute lesson related to our current genre study. Students then work independently on an ongoing writing project. Meet with students to assess their projects or review specific skills that will help them develop as writers. At the end of the writing workshop, one or two students share their work with the class.

Visit Vault at **www.vault.com** for insider company profiles, expert advice, career message boards, expert resume reviews, the Vault Job Board and more.

VAULT CAREER LIBRARY   85

10:15 a.m.:	Escort students to art class. Prep period; use this time to prepare for afternoon math class, something that involves making copies of worksheets or assessments (tests), and collecting materials needed for math games.
11:00 a.m.:	Lunch—take students to cafeteria and then eat lunch while checking homework folders for completed assignments and notes from parents.
11:50 a.m.:	Pick up students from recess. It takes about 10 minutes for class to file back inside and upstairs to the fourth floor.
12:00 p.m.:	Class meeting; followed by 10 to 15 minutes of "quiet time" for students, when they can do a quiet activity of their choice such as drawing or reading. During quiet time, meet with several students who have behavior plans that we review together on a daily basis.
12:20 p.m.:	Teach first grade math class. Work with first graders from two different classes while second graders go to another teacher for math. Instruction consists of a short lesson followed by work time. During work time, go to each table of students and assist them with any problems. End with a short meeting to review the day's work.
1:20 p.m.:	Read aloud to class.
1:30 p.m.:	Snack.
1:45 p.m.:	Reading classes. Due to the large range of student ages and skills in the class, students are divided into five different reading groups. During reading time, work with one group of students on skills specific to their reading level, while the other students read independently from books at their reading levels.
2:15 p.m.:	Social studies lesson.
2:45 p.m.:	Prepare for dismissal. Students gather belongings and line up. Review daily behavior plans with students, completing a feedback page that these students are required to take home to their parents.

3:00 p.m.:	Dismiss students to parents, caregivers, school buses or after-school programs.
3:15 p.m.:	Check mailbox and clean up classroom.
3:45 p.m.:	Planning, meeting and filing time. Plan lessons, prepare materials, file assessments and make copies. Depending on the day, there may be a staff meeting or a meeting with a mentor teacher scheduled during this time.
5:30 p.m.:	Commute.
6:30 p.m.:	Arrive home. Spend time responding to e-mails from parents and co-workers throughout the evening.

Middle School

Middle school students are notoriously challenging to work with, but teachers who enjoy this age group find it incredibly rewarding. Children this age are impressionable, and as a result, many middle school educators feel that they have the opportunity to make a big difference in children's lives.

Middle school students

During early adolescence, children develop a much greater capacity for abstract thought, a greater ability for self-reflection, and an ability to make complex inferences based on their existing knowledge. This increased capacity for higher thought makes children this age intensely curious. In school, they are extremely interested in applying the things that they learn to real-life situations; a good middle school teacher will be skilled at helping students to make these connections. At the same time, students this age are easily distracted by their peers and are very focused on social relationships.

Trends and cliques

In fact, the importance of social relationships to students this age cannot be overstated. They are often preoccupied with following trends and adopting the clothing, music preferences and hobbies of their friends. It is important for children this age to feel accepted by peers, and they frequently worry about being "normal." To get the attention of their classmates, many students will

Visit Vault at **www.vault.com** for insider company profiles, expert advice, career message boards, expert resume reviews, the Vault Job Board and more.

VAULT CAREER LIBRARY   **87**

disrupt the class with jokes or other silly behavior. Middle school students often form cliques, and they may spend a great deal of energy discussing whom they should include in social activities, and whom to exclude.

As students place more emphasis on relationships with peers, they distance themselves from family members, particularly their parents. At the same time, children this age typically adopt the values and moral positions of their parents, and other adults who they admire. They are interested in exploring ethical questions and tend to have a strong sense of justice.

Students this age resent being "treated like children," and are often eager to share their thoughts and opinions with adults—particularly adults outside of their families. However, despite the desire to be taken seriously by adults, middle school students frequently challenge the authority of their teachers.

Physical development

During middle school, most children enter puberty. Girls tend to develop more quickly than boys, but there is a wide range of physical development among children this age. This is stressful to many children, particularly those who develop earlier or later than their peers. They also begin to show more interest in the opposite sex, and are frequently preoccupied with their physical appearance.

Middle school students are moody. Their self-esteem fluctuates constantly, as they try to figure out who they are and to identify their role within a peer group. They also frequently vacillate between acting like adults and acting like children. Although they often view themselves as adults, when sick, frightened, upset, or otherwise under stress, they may become very childish.

For many children, early adolescence is a happy time, but it can also be a confusing time. Students this age are constantly reflecting on themselves and trying to figure out their place in the world. At the same time, they begin to ask themselves unanswerable questions about life and death, and they often find these thoughts frightening and overwhelming.

Teaching middle school

In middle school, students begin to travel to different classes, and to teachers who are experts in each subject. In some schools, students in fifth and sixth grade stay in one classroom with an elementary-certified teacher, while seventh and eighth graders move between classes. This helps ease the transition between elementary and middle school—a shift many students find difficult.

At the middle school level students are expected to take greater responsibility for their learning. For example, they usually have lockers and are held responsible for bringing the books and supplies they need to each class. They also may be given more long-term independent projects.

Finding a balance

To successfully work with middle school students, teachers need to find the right balance between giving students some freedom while at the same time providing a structured learning environment. One way that a middle school teacher can accomplish this is by giving students a choice of different assignments. For example, an English teacher might allow students to write an essay on one of three different topics, each of which relates to a different theme of a novel. This allows students to take some control over their own learning, while at the same time keeping them focused on the lesson's learning objectives.

Classroom management

Classroom management is extremely important at the middle school level. Children this age will frequently "test" the teacher. If a middle school classroom is not well-managed, students will quickly fall into inappropriate behaviors. It's important to recognize that classroom management is more than just discipline; simply by providing students with a well-organized, structured environment, a teacher can prevent many behavioral problems. However, no matter how well-organized a classroom is, every middle school teacher will need to be stern with students from time to time— especially at the beginning of the school year when students are eager to test the limits of their new teachers.

Steve Tullin, who has mentored dozens of middle school teachers and once taught middle school himself, says that at the middle school level, capturing the students' attention is critical. "You have to use lots of bells and whistles when you're teaching middle school. You employ specific literacy strategies—and although these strategies are also useful in high school, at the high school level you don't have to use them all the time. It's much harder to engage the interest of middle school students, and the teacher really has to be a performer."

At the middle school level, teachers typically have less planning work than elementary school teachers, because they often teach the same lesson to different groups of students.

Grading papers

At the middle school level, grading papers also becomes a bigger job because students complete longer, more complicated assignments. And these papers and tests are completed by multiple groups of students. For example, a teacher who has five sections of seventh grade English and assigns a five-page paper to his classes will have as many as 150 papers to read.

Multiple subjects

In very small schools, teachers may be expected to teach multiple subjects to students at multiple grade levels, rather than different sections of the same subject. This places an enormous workload on the teacher, because of the more advanced academic content at this level. Jim Tileston, who works at a small Catholic school, teaches English, social studies, religion and art to a split-level class of fifth and sixth graders, and English and social studies to a split-level class of seventh and eighth graders. "It's extremely difficult," he says. "It doesn't matter if you're preparing a lesson for five students or thirty students—it's the same amount of work. Some days I have to prepare twelve different lessons because I'm covering so much material with so many different grade levels."

However, Tileston says he enjoys working with students at a wide range of age levels because it gives him a chance to watch them grow up. "There's a huge change between fifth graders and eighth graders in terms of how they communicate, how they behave and how they view themselves. What I enjoy about the fifth and sixth graders is their energy. As long as I get them to harness that energy, they can do amazing things. With seventh and eighth graders what I really like is the way they're a little more jaded. They have a much better understanding of the world, and they can talk about issues in a way that the younger kids can't."

A Day In the Life: Middle School Teacher

After finishing his undergraduate education with a degree in theater and history, Jim Tileston worked for several years as a lighting designer. Although he enjoyed this line of work, he was drawn to the teaching profession because he felt that it was a stable career choice and an opportunity to make a difference in the lives of children.

Jim enrolled in a master's with certification program and commuted into Chicago from his home in Oak Park, Illinois. After graduating from his master's program, Jim found that it was difficult to find employment, because the public schools in his area—some of the most competitive in the country—rarely hire people straight out of master's with certification programs. At the same time, while there is a great need for teachers in the Chicago schools, city laws state that all public school teachers must be residents of the city itself. So Jim worked for some time as a substitute teacher, until he found a job at a Catholic school in a working-class suburb.

Two grades at a time

Because his school is so small, nearly all of the classes consist of students at two grade levels. While it's a lot of work to teach split-level courses, Jim feels that the size of the school provides a personal environment which is particularly valuable for middle school students. "For the middle school grades, a smaller school is very valuable. There's a real value in every kid having a place in the school, for every kid having a voice and being recognized daily. Because my school goes from pre-K through grade eight, there's also an excellent value in having the older kids work with the younger kids, doing peer mentoring. This creates a legacy, it gives the younger kids a sense of where they're going, and it makes the older kids feel affirmed about what they know and what they have to offer."

The Catholic setting

Jim believes that the role of religion in where he currently teaches is greater than it is at most Catholic schools. "In our school religion is ever-present. I was raised in Catholic school settings, so I have other schools I can compare ours to. This one is a lot more religious in the sense that the students are more involved in daily prayer than at some other Catholic schools. We're attached to a parish that is particularly conservative, and we go to church every week, whereas at some Catholic schools you go once a month. We spend a fair amount of time on religion-based activities. As much as possible I'm expected to integrate references to Jesus Christ into the curriculum, no matter what subject I'm teaching. For example, if I'm teaching civil rights I should mention that Martin Luther King was a Christian minister. Religion is ever present, but doesn't get in the way of things. Almost all the kids in our school are being sent there by their parents because they think we will be reinforcing their religious beliefs. That is the expectation."

Visit Vault at **www.vault.com** for insider company profiles, expert advice, career message boards, expert resume reviews, the Vault Job Board and more.

VAULT CAREER LIBRARY   **91**

The ESL element

Many of Jim's students speak Spanish as a first language. This has given Jim the opportunity to improve his own Spanish-language skills, which is something that he has enjoyed. He believes that it is important to acknowledge the importance of Spanish language in his students' lives. "I do a lot with trying to point out connections between English and Spanish words so that my students can see that the languages are interrelated. I also give my students a great amount of freedom to read and write in Spanish— if they can't read and write in their native language they will have trouble reading and writing English. My students who are the best readers in English are also the ones who can read and write well in Spanish."

When possible, Jim speaks Spanish to parents who have little fluency in English. Although his Spanish is sometimes a little rusty, he says, "I mostly feel comfortable going through teacher-parent conferences in Spanish. And the parents are forgiving, thank goodness, if I don't use the proper verb tense."

The strong sense of community at Jim's school is something that he believes is special—and that he believes is a contributing factor to the academic success of his students. "A lot of the kids in our school have been removed from large public schools for one reason or another. And I think that their success at our school is not due to the individual teachers as much as the small environment. It gives the students space to be themselves, and it gives us more control for setting boundaries."

A day in Jim's life

5:30 a.m.:   Wake up. Get dressed, eat, check e-mail.

7:00 a.m.:   Leave for school, the drive takes 20 minutes.

7:20 a.m.:   Arrive at school and complete the following routine:

1. Open the classroom.

2. Write the date and other pertinent information on the chalkboard.

3. Check the coatroom for any mess, and clean up if necessary.

4. Straighten desks.

5. Make copies or prep lessons for the morning.

6. Hand out papers, placing them on students' desks.

7:45 a.m.:   Staff meeting and prayer.

8:00 a.m.:   Return to the classroom to welcome students, unless assigned to supervise the parking lot that morning.

8:05 a.m.:   Morning "start up." Call rows of students to go to coatroom. Take attendance and handle any other business that needs to be addressed with the class.

8:15 a.m.:   Give students a "Number Enigma," a math puzzle that will help students wake up.

8:30 a.m.:   Teach religion to grades five and six, using the same curriculum for both grades.

9:15 a.m.:   Teach English to grades five and six, using separate curriculum and separate lessons for the two different grades.

10:05 a.m.:   Planning period; fifth and sixth grade students are at computer class

10:50 a.m.:   Teach literature, using two different lessons for grades five and six. If it's a Tuesday, students use this period for silent reading.

11:25 a.m.:   Recess. Eat lunch and prep for afternoon classes.

11:45 p.m.:   Students return to the classroom to eat lunch. Set up for the afternoon classes while the students eat.

12:05 p.m.:   Switch classes—grades five and six go to another teacher for their math and science instruction. Grades seven and eight arrive for English/history instruction. Teach seventh and eighth grade English, using separate curricula and lessons for the two grades.

12:50 p.m.:   Teach seventh and eighth grade History, using separate curricula and separate lessons for the two grades.

1:35 p.m.:   Classes switch back. Teach spelling to grades five and six, using separate curricula and lessons for the two grades.

Visit Vault at **www.vault.com** for insider company profiles, expert advice, career message boards, expert resume reviews, the Vault Job Board and more.

VAULT CAREER LIBRARY

93

2:15 p.m.:	Afternoon announcements. Students prepare to go home.
2:25 p.m.:	Dismissal.
2:45 p.m.:	Grade papers, clean, prepare lessons for next day.
4:00 p.m.:	Leave school to coach the basketball team. (During the season, practice is held twice a week.) Open up the gym for students who want extra practice time.
5:00 p.m.:	Basketball practice.
6:30 p.m.:	Drive home.
7:00 p.m.:	Have dinner and spend time with family.
10:00 p.m.:	Go to bed.

High School

High school students

High school students see themselves as adults and have a strong desire to act independently. As they grow out of early adolescence, their behavior becomes more consistently mature. At this age, the acceptance of their peers continues to be important, but at the same time, they begin to value and accept the things that make them different.

High school students have a greater ability to work independently than younger children. Although they continue to need some classroom structure, they can be expected to complete certain tasks with minimal adult supervision. They also have longer attention spans than younger children, and can be expected to sit and work quietly on their assignments.

Thinking about the future

During high school, students begin to think seriously about colleges and career possibilities. They also begin to understand the impact of their grades on the future, which may result in a feeling of pressure to perform academically. As they move towards the first adult decisions of their lives, high school students are likely to seek the advice of adults.

As students move through high school, the wide range of physical maturity levels closes up, with most students entering puberty and reaching their adult heights. As they grow into their adult bodies, many students become preoccupied with their own body images. They also grow into a more adult understanding of their own sexuality, and often begin seriously dating. As they reach more adult maturity levels, they become capable of entering into meaningful romantic relationships.

High school students have a great capacity for abstract thinking; they are capable of adult reasoning and advanced intellectual thought. This is often demonstrated through an increased interest in national and world events.

Teaching high school

People who teach high school enjoy the students' maturity and ability to complete advanced academic work. Because many people enjoy working with this age group, the job market for high school teaching positions is more difficult than at lower grade levels. This is particularly true for English and social studies teachers, with less competition for the high needs areas of math science, and special needs.

Honors and AP

By high school, students at most schools are "tracked" by academic skill level. Honors and advanced placement courses have the most academically gifted students, and, in most cases, experienced, tenured teachers teach these upper-level courses, while new teachers are given remedial or middle-level classes. Honors classes are considered desirable because the students are typically motivated, well-behaved and capable of college-level academic work. Brigid Tileston, who teaches some advanced placement courses, says that at this level the focus is more intensely academic. "When you go into teaching you think 'everybody loves Shakespeare like I do,' or 'everyone loves to read and write.' Then you discover that the job is more about connecting with the kids, for sure. Teaching advanced placement English in the type of school where I teach, the focus really is on the curriculum. It's both that and showing the kids that you care. I'm lucky to teach those types of classes."

However, Tileston says that even at the honors level, it still can be a challenge to keep students engaged, "Motivation is still an issue," she says, "but to a much lesser degree. There are some students who are just taking advanced placement classes to get into a good college. There are some

Visit Vault at www.vault.com for insider company profiles, expert advice, career message boards, expert resume reviews, the Vault Job Board and more.

VAULT CAREER LIBRARY   95

students who are great but don't do their daily homework. These students aren't failing, but they're also not achieving at the level they could."

Expertise required

However, in order to teach an upper-level course, a teacher must truly be an expert in the subject area, and capable of dealing with highly intelligent students who may question her expertise. Communicating with parents of students in top-level courses can also be a challenge—many teachers have stories of parents questioning their child's grade and the teacher's knowledge and authority. Tileston says that this is the biggest disadvantage of teaching in a wealthy suburban community. "Sometimes the parents are overly involved, which can have a downside. They feel that as taxpayers they can dictate the curriculum. I don't really have any horror stories, but I've heard them from other teachers."

Teachers at the high school level have the opportunity to teach specialized courses. For example, a high school English teacher might teach American literature, British literature, speech, debate, creative writing or drama. And a math teacher might teach geometry, algebra or calculus. In wealthy, high-performing school districts there is likely to be a greater variety of course offerings than in low-performing schools. In those schools that are labeled as "failing," there may be an emphasis on basic literacy and math skills, even at the high school level.

The paper load

At the high school level, paper grading is an enormous amount of work. As in middle school, the sheer number of students dictates that a teacher will have to grade many papers for each project that is assigned; as students become more academically advanced, these assignments are likely to become longer and more involved.

Tileston says, "For me, right now, having taught for ten years, the biggest challenge is the paper load outside of school. As a teacher you have wonderful vacations, but you also always have a stack of papers on your desk that you could be grading." However, while grading remains a challenge, she says that she has discovered some strategies for managing her workload. "Definitely use a rubric, even if it takes more time because this helps you be decisive in creating a grade. Also create benchmark papers with other teachers who are teaching the same class. Have each teacher look at three random papers, and then explain what grade they'd give and why. It also helps to focus on a few specific things in your grading, and to tell your students what you plan to focus on. This is especially helpful if you're teaching a lower-level class. Sometimes if you mark everything that's wrong with a paper, the kids don't get much out of it. A lot of kids will just shut down if you give them a paper that's dripping in red ink."

Debbie Beaudin, who teaches freshman English in Queens, New York, keeps portfolios of each of her students' work, because she finds that this helps her monitor their writing progress. "My school started requiring us to keep a writing portfolio for every class. This is something that I actually have found helpful. I have a portfolio for every kid and I update it every other marking period. The students have a reflection that they staple to each assignment where they evaluate how they think they did on the assignment, and say what they could have done better, and how the teacher could have helped them better. So at the end of the year they have about 20 writing assignments with these reflections."

Intellectual rewards

Tileston says that the opportunity to lead a high school drama department, combined with the maturity level of students in their upper teens, is what drew her to the high school level. "I am also certified in middle school, but I chose high school because at that level you can get into more specialized subject matter. You still need to motivate your students, but you can also have higher-level discussions with them. Kids that age can make inferences, they can make connections between literature and their own lives, or literature and politics."

A Day in the Life: High School Teacher

Debbie Beaudin began her teaching career as an adjunct professor at a community college in Gainesville, Florida. In this position Debbie taught remedial English to students who did not yet qualify for English 101. After several years, she moved to New York City, and found a job working for an organization that does post-graduate training for lawyers. Although Debbie was glad to find another job within the realm of education, she missed working in the classroom. In her spare time, she did volunteer tutoring at a housing project near her home in Queens.

The "a-ha" moment

Debbie can pinpoint one particular experience that helped her make the decision to become a high school English teacher. "This one kid was studying vocabulary words, and he was supposed to use them in sentences. I started

Visit Vault at **www.vault.com** for insider company profiles, expert advice, career message boards, expert resume reviews, the Vault Job Board and more.

VAULT CAREER LIBRARY

97

talking to him about the words—one of the words was 'flamboyant' and I said 'do you know what that means?' He told me that he didn't. So then I gave him a scenario that really represented the word. I said, 'I'm wearing a leopard print coat and I have leopard shoes and I get into my car, which has stripes on it.' He really got the words when I started talking to him about them. He understood the words one hundred percent by the time I left, and he probably understood them one percent when I got there. This was an experience that made me think I'd really like being a teacher. At the same place I tutored a second grader, but I didn't like working with her as much because I didn't really know what she was supposed to be able to do. She'd write a paragraph and I didn't know if it was a good paragraph for a second grader, or if it was a below average paragraph for a second grader. For high school, I knew that the sky was the limit, and I realized that working with high school students was most exciting and stimulating for me."

After joining the New York City Teaching Fellows program, Debbie was placed at a large public high school with several thousand students. Despite the current movement towards small schools, Debbie says that she enjoys working in a large school. "There's a feeling of excitement. There is always so much going on. There are tons of after-school activities, and there are always a lot of people around. The school is predominately English language learners, and they really feel like it's their school, which is great."

Debbie enjoys working with English language learners, but she says that it poses certain challenges. "There are students at all different levels, and you can't assume that the students know any words. Many of the kids speak Spanish at home, and they speak Spanish with their friends. The only place they're getting exposure to the English language is at school. That makes it more difficult for them to develop good English reading and writing skills."

Like many English teachers, Debbie often finds the task of grading papers overwhelming. She's found that the best way to manage this task is to grade papers frequently, for small amounts of time. For example, she often grades papers on the subway as she commutes to work.

Learning from other staff

Debbie recommends that new teachers make an effort to form bonds with co-workers. "Find a master teacher in your school, someone who will help you, someone you feel comfortable around. Try to find that person and observe their classes. I had a teacher like that and she was great. She let me visit her classes, she talked to me about lessons, and she gave me advice and ideas. I could tell her anything. When you start teaching, look around and you'll know who the master teachers are—they're not part of a clique, and they're not the people who are cynical all the time. Also, be friendly to everyone. Some people start teaching and they go around like they know everything, but you need to be willing to learn from other teachers."

A day in Debbie's life

6:45 a.m.:	Wake up.
7:45 a.m.:	Leave for work.
8:45 a.m.:	Arrive at work. Spend some time running around doing last-minute preparations for the day—get copies, check mail, get the attendance envelope from the office.
9:12 a.m.:	Single period ninth grade English class.
10:05 a.m.:	Planning period—locate materials, make an "agenda" poster for the double-period reading classes, order books, pick up copies from the copy room.
10:50 a.m.:	Double-period ninth grade English class.
12:30 p.m.:	Lunch. Take 20 minutes completely "off" to eat lunch. Spend the next 20 minutes doing paperwork like grading and record keeping.
1:10 p.m.:	Double-period ninth grade English class.
3:00 p.m.:	Tutor students in school library.
4:00 p.m.:	Leave school.
5:00 p.m.:	Arrive home.

In the evening: Spend one hour planning the next day's lessons and another hour grading student assignments.

Visit Vault at **www.vault.com** for insider company profiles, expert advice, career message boards, expert resume reviews, the Vault Job Board and more.

V/\ULT CAREER LIBRARY   99

Higher Education

Students in higher education

Students at universities—whether in graduate or undergraduate programs—may span a large age range. Typically, students begin undergraduate programs around age 18 and complete their schooling four years later, but at many universities there is a significant percentage of students who are much older.

Whatever age college students are, students in an institution of higher learning are expected to take responsibility for their own education. A good college professor will give personal attention to students who request it, but students are expected to do much of their work independently and to behave as adults in the classroom.

Keeping motivation alive

Despite the maturity of their students, college professors, like any other teachers, sometimes struggle to keep students motivated. This can be particularly challenging in undergraduate classes, because students at this level are required to take courses in a variety of academic disciplines, some of which may not be interesting to them. To address this, many universities offer courses such as "physics for non-scientists" and "English for engineers," which are geared towards students who are fulfilling their liberal arts requirements in an area outside of their primary interest.

While the expectation is that college students are ready for advanced-level academic work, many professors believe that too many students enter college without basic academic skills. And, although this may be truer in "non-competitive" colleges with open enrollments, teachers at top universities also encounter students who need remedial instruction.

Students who enter a traditional college immediately after completing high school often find themselves away from home and adult supervision for the first time in their lives. This is an adjustment for many students; some become homesick and depressed, while others focus on the thrills of independent living to the detriment of their academic progress.

Teaching higher education

Within the academic community, there is an expectation that people enter academia because they are focused on their intellectual specialty area. And, indeed, a teaching job in higher education offers the opportunity to focus on a highly specific subject area.

Many academics, while required to teach courses, are more interested in their own research and writing than they are in teaching, and many university hiring committees downplay the teaching aspects of a professorship. Instead of looking for good teachers, they look for people with advanced degrees and extensive publications under their belts, which is why the maxim "publish or perish" is often used to describe the academic climate. Despite this, most universities do collect student evaluations of professors, and value the contributions of charismatic teachers who make a difference in their students' lives.

Authority in the classroom

Although at the university level, student behavior is less of a concern than at the K-12 level, it is important for a teacher of adult education to maintain authority in the classroom. Sam Jordan, an assistant law professor, says he sometimes finds it difficult to keep his students' attention. "The students all have laptops, and they get on the internet during class. Lots of times they'll laugh when you haven't said anything funny. This is not a problem with my first-year classes, but with my second-year students it's more of a problem. For this reason, some professors want to ban laptops from the classrooms. It's an issue that comes up a lot in discussions of legal education, and something law teachers like to complain about."

Debbie Beaudin says that she had very few disciplinary problems when teaching at the college level. "In a community college, the students are a lot more motivated than high school students. There is very little classroom disruption or classroom management issues. I only had one disruption when I was teaching community. A student was interrupting me in class, so I just very quietly said 'I'd love to talk to you more about that after class— right now I'm talking about something else,' and that worked beautifully. When you're teaching children they have a lot less self-control. You can't expect them to act like adults because they're not."

Outside the classroom

Compared to teachers of younger grade levels, professors spend relatively little time in the classroom. They may only teach three or four classes, each of which meets two or three times a week. When not in the classrooms, professors host "office hours" (times that they have reserved for meetings with students), they work on their own research and writing, and they serve on university committees. Involvement in university committees is something that can be very time-consuming. New professors, in particular,

Visit Vault at **www.vault.com** for insider company profiles, expert advice, career message boards, expert resume reviews, the Vault Job Board and more.

VAULT CAREER LIBRARY   **101**

often feel pressured to serve on these committees because this is seen as part of the road to tenure.

Freedoms

While basic Freshman 101-type courses often follow a prescribed curriculum, college professors often have the freedom to design their own courses. They typically do not turn in daily lesson plans to school administrators—although they are required to have their syllabi approved before the beginning of an academic term. As at the K-12 levels, university professors are often observed and evaluated, most often by senior members of the faculty. Jordan says that his university has a "pretty aggressive monitoring process. People come in and observe my lectures, but it's friendly."

The paper-grading responsibilities of an educator in higher education vary widely. College-level courses often have few graded assignments each semester—although these assignments may be extremely long papers that are time-consuming to read. Remedial, lower-level classes are more likely to have weekly graded assignments than honors-level and graduate courses. In universities with large, lecture-style courses, professors frequently have teaching assistants (TAs). These are usually graduate students who lead break-out sections of the class and are responsible for the majority of the grading, leaving the senior professor free to spend time on other pursuits.

Getting in

Entry into the field of academia is extremely competitive. Many people obtain PhDs with the intention of going into academia only to find themselves without a job after graduation. Anyone considering a career in academia should be open to the possibility of relocating to another part of the country if this is what it takes to find a job.

The job market for university professors is competitive in part due to the fact that, to save costs, many universities rely heavily on "adjunct" professors—people who are hired to teach one or two courses but who are not full-time members of the staff. Adjunct professors do not have health insurance, access to pension plans, or other benefits awarded to full-time faculty. Many people teaching in an adjunct capacity find it frustrating not to be able to find full-time work after spending years of time and thousands of dollars working towards an advanced degree. However, despite its disadvantages, teaching in an adjunct capacity can be a good way to break into academia.

Teaching positions at the community college level are often easier to obtain than positions at prestigious, four-year universities. Debbie Beaudin says that she was able to obtain a position as a community college professor immediately after finishing college because "you needed a bachelor's, not a master's, which was perfect. They were looking for someone with good writing skills."

Tenure

While the job market is tough at the higher education level, most universities award tenure to teachers after they have worked full time for several years. Once they earn tenure, college professors have a great deal of job stability. It is rare for a tenured professor to be fired or laid off.

Nowadays, many people who are serious about a career in academia earn PhDs in multiple subject areas to make themselves more competitive. For example, someone with an interest in Victorian literature might earn a PhD in English and a PhD in history. The amount of time it takes to obtain dual PhDs is, of course, extensive—and something that may not seem realistic to every would-be professor. However, in today's academic climate, it is a way to get noticed by university hiring committees.

Notes from the field

Debbie Beaudin says that compared to her current responsibilities as a high school teacher, teaching community college was easy. "The workload at the high school level is a lot greater. At the college level students were given fewer assignments—at the high school level the grading is much more overwhelming."

Sam Jordan, who taught fourth grade for two years before going to law school and becoming a professor, agrees that the workload of a professors is very different from the workload of a K-12 teacher. "When I was in Teach for America, I spent most of every day in the classroom teaching. Now I teach three days a week for two 60-minute periods each day. So the time I spend in the classroom is a lot less. I also spend a lot less time grading than I did when teaching elementary school. This year I've spent a lot of time prepping for my classes. I'm in the classroom less, but I spend more time preparing than I did when I was teaching K-12. I also have office hours, and meetings with students, or they sometimes just drop by. I also go to faculty workshops, and serve on faculty committees. My days are a lot more unstructured. But I work probably the same number of hours."

Graduate teaching

Jordan found his full-time job as a law professor after doing a fellowship at Harvard Law School, and he says that this route into academia is one that he would recommend. "Getting into law teaching in some respects is easier than getting into other fields like English, but there still aren't tons of positions. I kind of lucked into it. I got it in my mind that I was going to go into teaching, and in the meantime I was working for a judge who got a letter from Harvard Law School asking him to recommend people for a fellowship. I got into teaching through that fellowship. It was designed explicitly for people who are interested in teaching. A lot of law schools are developing fellowships, and there are also post-doc programs for people who want to teach higher education. It's totally possible to get into teaching in unorthodox ways, but there are things you can do that are extremely valued, things that can be helpful if you're trying to break into the field, and a fellowship is one of them."

Now, as a member of his law school hiring committee, Jordan says that he looks for people who will become valuable members of the academic community. "The best piece of advice I ever got is that during an interview you want to convince people that you'd be a good colleague. You shouldn't try to be flashy, but you should act like you're already part of the club. That's what people are looking for. They're thinking 'how would this person be to work with?' 'Would this be a good person to have lunch with and talk to about my research?' We think about how this person will be in a classroom full of students."

Jordan also says that while he doesn't think his experiences teaching elementary school helped him find a job teaching law school, they did help him become a better teacher of law. "There are definitely things I learned from teaching fourth grade that I've imported into teaching law school. When I started my fellowship, people would joke about how I went from teaching fourth grade to teaching Harvard law students. I would say, sort of glibly, 'It's not as different as you think,' but it's true. There are skills you can develop as a teacher that are relevant in any area. I think I'm a better teacher for having that experience."

Specialty Areas within the Field of Education

CHAPTER 11

In addition to the core academic subjects (English, math, science, social studies and international languages) there are a number of specialty content areas within the field of education. The professionals who work in these areas are important members of every school community, and they play a significant role in ensuring that the academic and emotional needs of all students are addressed.

Teaching Special Needs Students

The term "special needs" refers to students who need specialized support due to physical, emotional or developmental disabilities. To become certified in special needs, teachers must complete extensive coursework that prepares them to understand the educational needs students with a wide range of abilities. The daily experiences of a special needs teacher vary, depending on the particular needs of the students in the classroom. Classes of special needs students are typically grouped by their needs and ability to function. For example, some special needs teachers might work exclusively with students who have emotional disabilities that result in severe behavioral issues; others work with students who have learning disabilities; others work with students who have physical disabilities, such as blindness.

Speech therapists are another, specialized type of special needs teacher. They work with students who have delays in their speech development and who may not have a disability. At the same time, many students with developmental delays and auditory impairments are likely to have speech delays, and frequently spend time with a speech therapist. In most cases, speech therapists work with students one-on-one to help them improve their pronunciation and enunciation techniques.

In a special needs classroom, teachers usually work with smaller groups of students than do regular education teachers. In many states, special education classes are classified according to the student-teacher ratio. For

Visit Vault at **www.vault.com** for insider company profiles, expert advice, career message boards, expert resume reviews, the Vault Job Board and more.

VAULT CAREER LIBRARY   105

example, a 12 to 1 class would have twelve students and one teacher. An 8 to 1 class would have eight students and one teacher.

Paraprofessionals

Most self-contained special needs classrooms (classrooms where the students remain for the entire day, as opposed to special needs classrooms where students spend only a part of their day) have one or more "paraprofessionals." These are adults who assist the teacher in the classroom. They are not trained teachers, but often are very experienced in the classroom setting and can be of great assistance. The number of paraprofessionals in a classroom is usually determined by the classification of a special needs class. For example, a 12 to 1 to 2 class would have twelve students, one teacher and two paraprofessionals. In some cases, children with severe disabilities or behavioral problems have their own paraprofessionals who are assigned to be with them at all times. Therefore, a 12 to 1 to 2 class might have the two paraprofessionals assigned to the class at large, and a third paraprofessional who is assigned to one particular student.

Resource rooms

Education law in most of the country states that special needs students must be placed in "the least restrictive environment" in which they can learn effectively. As a result, many students receive specialized academic support while spending some of the time in "mainstream" classes. Many schools have "resource rooms" for students who spend most of their time in regular classes but who need specialized support. Students may go to the school resource room for one particular subject, such as math, or for a specified number of class hours each week.

Some resource room teachers work with students in a variety of different academic areas. Others focus on a specific content area, such as "reading specialists" who work with students on literacy skills. In some situations, reading specialists will also work as "push in" teachers, visiting classrooms during literacy instruction and working with students in the class who need extra assistance.

Inclusion classes

In recent years, "inclusion" classes have become common in special needs education. An inclusion class is one in which some of the students are in regular education, while others have learning disabilities. In an inclusion class, there is one regular-education teacher and one special needs teacher.

All students in the class generally follow a regular education curriculum, but those with learning disabilities are given extra support, and modified assignments (or graded using a modified rubric) as necessary.

In both inclusion classrooms and self-contained classrooms with paraprofessionals, special needs teachers must be able to work closely with the other adults in the classroom. Most teachers at the K-12 level spend most of their time alone with their students, but special needs teachers are frequently in classrooms where there are other adults in the classroom at all times. This can be a great advantage to the teacher and the students; it is an opportunity to share observations on students' progress, to provide students with individualized instruction, and to cooperatively plan lessons. However, if the adults in a classroom are unwilling or unable to cooperate with one another, this can be an enormous source of stress for both the adults and the students.

A collaborative process

Chad Hamilton, who teaches a self-contained class of third, fourth and fifth graders, stresses the importance of building constructive relationships with paraprofessionals. "I make an effort to get the paras involved in academics as much as possible. A lot of paras I've worked with think that they're just there for when the kids act up, but they're there to facilitate learning. It can be difficult to get the paras involved, because you have to manage them. For some teachers I know, and even in my own experience to some extent, managing the paras can be more challenging than students, but they can be a tremendous resource. Its not that they don't want to be involved, it's that no one has told them how they can be involved. They don't feel empowered in the classroom, and I don't understand why that is. But it can be a difficult relationship, if the kids see that another adult in room doesn't respect you, they won't respect you either. I can't imagine it, but I've heard horror stories of screaming matches in the classroom."

Individual Education Plans

Individual Education Plans, commonly known as IEPs, are an essential component of special needs education. Every student who receives special needs services (or who is being considered for special needs services) is periodically evaluated by the school IEP committee. The evaluation process consists of tests that measure the child's development in all areas where special services are required. The makeup of an IEP committee depends on the types of services the student receives, but often consists of school social workers, psychiatrists, counselors, speech therapists and classroom teachers.

Visit Vault at **www.vault.com** for insider company profiles, expert advice, career message boards, expert resume reviews, the Vault Job Board and more.

VAULT CAREER LIBRARY   **107**

The evaluation committee determines that a student needs special services, then creating an IEP for that student, outlining the services that this student will receive and the goals that the student is expected to achieve over the course of the year. Throughout the school year, the IEP committee will assess the student's progress toward these goals.

Hamilton says that the paperwork involved in complying with students' IEPs is "pretty significant. We're assessing students on a daily basis. But this depends partly on the school and what expectations or demands of the administration are. We're expected to keep conference notes. Any time I confer with a student I'm expected to write down a detail about how they're working. I need to do that for every student every day, for reading and writing. And it's recommended for every subject. Plus, I have to fill out forms when a behavior issue occurs."

Like Hamilton, Rachel Wadle, who teaches in a preschool inclusion class, says, "Writing an IEP takes up some time. I have been writing them for a while now so, it takes less and less time depending on the kids and how many goals they have. I have to keep data weekly on each goal. Right now I have five kids on IEPs, and a total of 13 goals to keep data on weekly. It takes a lot of my week to get that data done. In their IEPs, I state that I will work with the kids 10 minutes a week per goal, which I can barely get done. Other paperwork also needs to be done. Some of my kids are Medicaid-billing kids and we have to fill out a paper every day on them to get paid for services they require, like taking them to the bathroom, feeding, and changing clothes."

The IEP process requires teachers to keep records documenting that the IEP is being conducted properly. It also requires teachers to document any significant incidents that take place in regards to students' behavior and/or academic progress. This is a time-consuming activity, and one that anyone going into the field of special needs education should be aware of.

Help wanted

In many districts throughout the country, special needs is considered a "high needs" subject area, meaning that there is a shortage of qualified instructors. In some areas this shortage is so severe that there are chronic special needs vacancies. And in competitive districts, it may be easier to find a position as a special needs teacher than in other subject areas.

Hamilton says that when he joined the New York City Teaching Fellows, he asked to be placed in a special needs environment. "It was something I wanted to do," he says. "When they asked me what population of students I wanted to teach, I chose to teach emotionally disturbed students in Brooklyn. My reason was that when I was tutoring this was the population I was predominantly working with. I really liked those kids and felt like I connected with them. While I was a tutor I would always think to myself, 'if I were the teacher I would try this.' I would fantasize about being their teacher. When the opportunity came along, I went with it. At the school where I tutored, so many of these students were suffering from not having good teachers. I would get angry about the lack of education they were receiving. And I wanted to make a difference where I thought they needed someone like me, and where I could make the biggest impact."

When working with students who have disabilities, it is important for a teacher to maintain a sense of perspective. "First and foremost, you need to have a good sense of humor," says Hamilton. "There are going to be things that happen that nobody can be prepared for, they're so ridiculous or almost surreal. All of my preconceptions about special education were completely surpassed within a couple weeks. There have been a lot of really intense situations. If you're not able to laugh about things—not to inappropriately laugh, but have a sense of humor and perspective about things—if you take it very, very seriously you're going to sink, you'll personalize things and fall prey to depression." You also need to "be able to establish a healthy distance between your teaching life and personal life."

Special needs students in mainstream classrooms

While some teachers work exclusively with special needs students, laws stating that special needs students be placed in the "least restrictive environment" guarantee that virtually every teacher will at some point work with students who receive special needs services (or at least every teacher in public education; private schools are not required to admit special needs students). Even in honors-level courses, teachers can expect to occasionally have students with a learning disability, such as dyslexia, or a physical disability. In some cases, it is easy for a teacher to meet the needs of a student who receives special needs services. For example, it might be a matter of seating a student with a hearing impairment in the front of the classroom. Students with learning disabilities may require more specific accommodations. For example, they may be given extra time to take exams, given modified assignments, or graded differently from the rest of the class. In these situations, a special needs teacher or the school IEP committee is usually responsible for communicating students' requirements to regular education teachers who teach these students.

Visit Vault at **www.vault.com** for insider company profiles, expert advice, career message boards, expert resume reviews, the Vault Job Board and more.

VAULT CAREER LIBRARY   **109**

In her speech and theater arts courses, Brigid Tileston typically has one or two students who spend most of their time in self-contained classrooms. These students often have serious developmental disabilities such as Down's syndrome, and she usually works with the special needs teacher to ensure that these students have a positive experience in her class. She also relies on the regular students in the class for support. "I talk to the class about it, and I ask the special education teacher to come in to talk to the class with me. I'm not worried that my kids will be mean, because they're really nice theater kids; but the other teacher will come in and the two of us will explain what the student is working on. Maybe they're working on social skills like shaking hands and calling people by name. In communications classes it's an opportunity to help the student learn to communicate better. We explain to the class that this student is being graded differently. Maybe they will do a 30- second monologue instead of a 5-minute monologue and they're working primarily on eye contact. It's good for the students to understand the types of interactions they can have with this student, and how they can help. It kind of breaks the ice too."

Teaching English Language Learners

Teachers of English language learners are responsible for helping students develop proficiency in the English language, as well as familiarizing them with the culture and customs of the United States. This means that, in addition to preparing students for academic instruction in English, teachers also prepare them for success in informal, social situations.

Until recently, the term "English as a second language" (or ESL) was used to describe students whose native language was something other than English. Now, however, the term "English language learner" (or ELL) is more commonly used. The term ESL has fallen out of favor because of the large number of students who are already fluent in multiple languages and learning English as a third or fourth language.

Specialized certification

ELL teachers must possess specialized certification in ELL instruction. To obtain this type of certification, teachers complete coursework that emphasizes the educational techniques that are most effective in teaching English to a non-native speaker. Many of these techniques involve presenting information in a variety of different ways (i.e., through written texts as well as visual illustrations), so that students have multiple opportunities to absorb the information being taught and to understand what the teacher expects of them.

The ELL classroom

Most ELL students spend the majority of their time in regular education classes and travel to an ELL classroom for a small portion of their day. The amount of time students spend in their ELL classroom is generally based upon their fluency in English and the amount of time they have been in the United States. In the past, ELL students spent much more time in specialized classrooms, but the current thinking is that immersion in a regular education classroom filled with native English speakers provides students with a motivation to develop fluency in the language.

ELL teachers spend most of their time working with small groups of students, with the exact student/teacher ratio dependent upon school or district policy and the fluency of the students in the classroom. One-on-one instruction may also be provided to students who are very new to the country and/or who have very little fluency in English.

Many ELL teachers are themselves fluent in multiple languages. Although not required, this is can be incredibly useful if the ELL population of a school predominately speaks one language, such as Spanish, and the teacher is also fluent in this language. However, ELL teachers are expected to have the necessary skills to teach children from anywhere in the world, and most teachers in pull-out ELL programs will at some point work with students who speak a language they are unfamiliar with.

Bilingual classrooms

While most ELL students attend "pull-out" ELL classes, in schools with large ELL populations there may also be bilingual classrooms. In these settings, students are taught in English for half the day and their native language for the other half. Bilingual classrooms are mostly designed for Spanish speakers, although there are also bilingual classes in the United States that teach students in Chinese, Russian, Haitian and a host of other languages.

The advantage of a bilingual classroom is that by instructing students in their native language, students are less likely to fall behind academically as they learn the English language. The disadvantage is that when all the students in a classroom speak the same non-English language, they are likely to speak predominately amongst themselves in their native language. Critics of bilingual education feel that students are better served through

Visit Vault at www.vault.com for insider company profiles, expert advice, career message boards, expert resume reviews, the Vault Job Board and more.

VAULT CAREER LIBRARY   111

placement in regular classrooms where they need to speak English in order to interact with their peers.

ELL challenges

One challenge for ELL teachers is to ensure that students do not fall behind academically as they adapt to a new culture and develop proficiency in English. This is a difficult task and one that must be accomplished by working with students' regular education teachers to ensure that the English language instruction reinforces the curriculum being taught in the students' other classes.

Whether working in a bilingual classroom or a pullout program, it is important for teachers to show cultural sensitivity towards ELL learners. These students need a command of English in order to succeed socially, academically and ultimately in the workplace; at the same time, teachers need to be aware of the pride and value that students place upon their native cultures and languages. By encouraging students to talk and write about their native countries, and showing an interest in their background and heritage, an ELL teacher can foster an English language learning environment where students do not feel as though they are being forced to give up their native language or culture.

As the immigrant population in the United States grows, ELL instruction is becoming a bigger and more important area within the sphere of education. In many regions of the country ELL overlaps with high-needs areas, so there are many job opportunities available for qualified teachers.

ESL in mainstream classrooms

Most regular education teachers will also work with students whose native language is something other than English. In some schools, the majority of the student population may be non-native English speakers.

To work effectively with English language learners, teachers need to "differentiate instruction," which refers to the process of tailoring classroom activities to the differing needs of individual students. To effectively differentiate instruction, a teacher might give students alternate assignments, grade them according to a different rubric, or take the time to re-explain assignments to them.

Debbie Beaudin, who teaches in a school with a large Spanish-speaking population, frequently teaches classes where some students barely speak English, whereas others are fluent. To address the differing needs of her students, she says, "I walk around a lot and give students individual attention—and I know who I need to go to first. Also, I clarify things that I know maybe 75 percent of the class won't need clarified, but I'll clarify them for the other 25 percent. I don't always clarify these things for the whole group, but I'll clarify it for the students who need extra help. Another thing I do is work with the seating arrangements. I know that if I sit certain kids together they'll help each other—even if I don't tell them to. It happens naturally."

ELL in other settings

There is a great deal of opportunity for ELL teachers outside of the K-12 environment. For example, many social service organizations and continuing education programs offer ELL services and need skilled ELL teachers. For the most part, teachers in these settings work with adult populations and are not required to have teacher certification. While the job qualifications of adult education ELL teachers are less rigorous than those of K-12 teachers, they are often paid lower salaries than public school teachers. For this reason, many certified ELL teachers prefer to work within the sphere of public education.

Clara Lin began her career as an ELL teacher for a social service organization, and says that it was a good way to explore her interest in a teaching career. Although she believes that ELL teachers in community organizations should be required to have more training, she says that her experiences with adult-level ELL inspired her to go back to school for a graduate degree in education.

Teaching Physical Education

Physical education teachers are usually certified to teach grades K-12. At the elementary level, they teach many groups of students each week, for one or two periods apiece. This gives the physical education teacher an opportunity to get to know many children in the school. At the same time, the teacher has less opportunity to become closely bonded with any one group of students.

At the secondary level, physical education teachers are more likely to teach five or six groups of students on a daily basis. In addition to teaching traditional "gym" classes, secondary physical education teachers often teach health courses. Typical gym courses also frequently have a health

Visit Vault at www.vault.com for insider company profiles, expert advice, career message boards, expert resume reviews, the Vault Job Board and more.

VAULT CAREER LIBRARY   113

component. For example, the curriculum for a personal fitness course might include a weekly nutrition lesson. While many students view physical education as a break from their academic routines, physical education is, in fact, an important part of students' education, and the physical education teacher is responsible for helping students to develop healthy habits that they will maintain throughout their lives. The importance of physical education has recently been recognized by many school districts. This has resulted in more stringent physical education curricula, and more emphasis on the life skills and healthy habits that students should take away from their physical education courses.

Many physical education teachers supplement their incomes by coaching high school athletic teams. This is usually not a job requirement, but for someone who is interested in sports this can be a rich and rewarding experience.

Teaching Art and Music

Like physical education teachers, art and music teachers are often certified to teach grades K-12. At the elementary school level, they often work with many different classes, while secondary teachers often work with a smaller pool of students.

At the secondary level, students usually choose to take art and music as electives, which means that teachers of these classes often have highly motivated groups of students in their classes.

Extracurricular requirements

Music teachers at the secondary level are often required to be involved in extracurricular activities. For example, a high school music teacher might be the leader of the school marching band. This is can be a significant time commitment, because it often requires after-school practices, and attendance at all of the high school's football games. At the same time, music teachers are paid for their involvement with extracurricular programs, and often find it extremely rewarding.

More competitive, less security

Teaching positions in art and music are often competitive due to large numbers of qualified applicants and a relatively small number of available positions. One caveat of a career teaching art or music at the K-12 level is that when school districts are forced to make budget cuts, art and music programs are often downsized or eliminated. In some areas of the country, this may mean that teachers in these subject areas have less job security than teachers in other subject areas. As a way of navigating both the competitive job market and the issue of job security, many people obtain dual certification in art or music and another core subject area.

There is a public awareness of the importance of music and art education, and many grants and other sources of public funding are available to schools hoping to expand their art and music programs. The process of applying for this type of grant can be time consuming, but there is funding available for schools that are willing to complete the paperwork.

Working as a School Media Specialist

The term "school librarian" has been replaced by the title of "media specialist." This is because in addition to exposing students to the traditional library resources, media specialists work extensively with computers and other new technologies. In most states, to become a school media specialist, you need at least two years of experience teaching in a regular classroom in addition to a master's of library science degree.

Job responsibilities

When a class of students visits a school library, the media specialist will often teach a lesson. This lesson (particularly at the younger grade levels) may involve reading a story or otherwise exposing students to different types of literature. Or the lesson may involve teaching students about how to conduct research, such as how to use the card catalog, or how to find information on the internet.

In addition to teaching lessons, a school media specialist is responsible for supervising classes that visit the library to work on research projects. This requires the media specialist to both monitor the behavior of students and to assist students who need help finding information.

A school media specialist will often have the opportunity to work with students who visit the library independently. These students may visit the library to get a break from the hustle and bustle of the school environment, to find information for a school project, or simply because they love to read. Whatever the case may be, this is an opportunity for students to explore the topics that interest them most, and for the school media specialist to nurture these interests.

Visit Vault at **www.vault.com** for insider company profiles, expert advice, career message boards, expert resume reviews, the Vault Job Board and more.

V/\ULT CAREER LIBRARY   **115**

A taste for technology?

In many schools, media specialists are expected to maintain the school's electronic equipment. For example, they may loan television sets and DVD players to classroom teachers. Or they may be responsible for monitoring and maintaining a computer lab. When media specialists take on these roles within the school setting, it is critical that they possess the technological skills to assist teachers and students with this type of equipment.

Over the past few years, rapidly expanding technologies have changed the role of the school librarian. In many schools, the media specialist is the person in the school community who is most "on the cutting edge" of new technologies. For someone with an interest in technology, research and literature, this can be a fascinating and rewarding career.

Working as a School Social Worker

School social workers address the social, emotional and academic issues that students face both at home and at school. To become a certified school social worker it is necessary to obtain a master's of social work (or in some states, a bachelor's of social work, although a master's is typically preferred). School social workers usually are not required to have teaching certification or experience in the classroom, although some of them do possess these requirements.

School social workers frequently do home visitations, working with an entire family to ensure the well-being of the child. This often involves working closely with the parents and other members of the household to create a living environment that will meet the child's needs. For example, a social worker might address hygiene issues, or distractions in the household that prevent the child from getting adequate rest at night or from finding a quiet place to study. When a child develops a problem such as an eating disorder or mental illness, the social worker will help parents to better understand the problem and to communicate with their child.

Because school social workers are intimately involved with entire families they frequently are asked to investigate situations where child abuse or neglect may be of concern. If they have reasonable suspicions that child abuse is taking place, they—like all educators—are responsible for reporting this to the proper authorities.

In recent years, school social workers have become increasingly involved in special needs education. They often serve as members of school IEP committees and help teachers and family members to better assist students achieve their educational goals. The involvement with special needs services often requires school social workers to complete extensive paperwork, in addition to establishing relationships with special needs students and their families.

Social workers will also meet one-on-one with the students on their caseloads. If, through these visits, the social worker determines that a student's needs are not being met either at school or at home, they will often refer the student to people who can help. This may involve having the child evaluated by an IEP committee, or finding community agencies that are willing to donate clothing, medical treatment or psychiatric care to the child.

The demands upon a school social worker are great, and social work can be an emotionally draining profession. At the same time, it can be a tremendously rewarding field for someone who cares about helping children and who has the ability to maintain a healthy perspective when dealing with difficult and sometimes upsetting situations.

Working as a School Counselor

Like school social workers, school counselors facilitate the social, emotional and academic well-being of students. However, school counselors do not usually conduct home visits and are less involved with students' families than school social workers (although they may meet with parents in the school setting).

To become a school counselor, you need to possess teaching certification, and an advanced degree in counseling is required in most states. Although not required by law, many schools also require school counselors to have several years of experience in the classroom because they believe that this facilitates good communication with the classroom teachers in the building.

Helping students cope

School counselors often work with students who are going through difficult transitional problems such as a death or divorce in the family. They also work with students who face serious and potentially dangerous situations at home or within the community, and like school social workers, they often play an important role in notifying the authorities when child abuse or neglect is suspected.

In addition to helping students who face serious, and sometimes dangerous, problems at home, school counselors work with students who have difficulties within the school environment. For example, they might meet with a student who refuses to do math assignments or a student who has trouble making friends. When school counselors suspect that problems at school are related to problems at home, they may refer a student to the school social worker. At this point, the social worker and counselor team up to make sure that the child's immediate needs are being met, and that the child has someone to talk to.

School counselors frequently work with groups of students. For example, if a group of students gangs up on another student, the counselor might meet with all of the students involved to help them work out their differences. Counselors also visit classrooms and teach lessons. These lessons may focus on academic issues (such as good study habits), social skills (such as conflict resolution) or social issues (such as peer pressure). The opportunity to work with both individual students and larger groups is something that many school counselors see as a benefit of the profession.

In schools with serious discipline problems, the school counselor may become an integral part of the schools' discipline process. Although counselors do not punish students, they are often asked to meet with students who are disruptive. While this can be an important contribution to the school community, school counselors need to be sure that they do not neglect well-behaved students because the behavior problems take up all their time. A student who sits quietly in the back of a classroom may need counseling services just as much as a student who misbehaves.

Getting into college

At the high school level, counselors are responsible for guiding students through the college admissions process. This involves speaking to groups of students about the college application process, meeting with them individually to help them decide which schools they will apply to and find financial aid, and writing letters of recommendation. In high schools with a large percentage of college-bound students, this may be the primary focus of the counselor's role within the school.

One counselor's experience

Betsy Sullivan became a school counselor after teaching elementary school and special education for a number of years in Ypsilanti, Michigan. Many of the students in her school came from a local housing project, and she believed that she could best help them in the role of school counselor. "I had students who would come to school without food, or they didn't have warm clothes, or they had to sleep on the floor all night because they were afraid of being shot. Stuff like that gets in the way, and it prevents students from learning. For students to be successful at learning, they need to get their emotional needs out of the way. As a counselor, you can't always do anything about students' home environment, but you can help them cope in ways that will allow them to focus in school."

Never the same day twice

Sullivan says that the unpredictability of the school counselor's routine was always something that she enjoyed—despite the fact that it was sometimes difficult to see children in emotional need. "As a counselor, you never know what your day will look like. You think it will look one way, and it ends up totally different. This can be kind of fun. However, it's difficult to see kids hurting because of the adults in their lives, or other factors that are outside their control. It can be very hard, very emotionally draining. So it's important to have something in your life that s a good stress reducer. But every single day, at least once a day, something would happen to make me glad I went to work that day."

More than one school

In many school districts, particularly at the elementary school level, one counselor may be assigned to work at two or more schools. This was the case for Sullivan. When she got a counseling job in a suburban community in Michigan, she was initially assigned to two different schools; when the district faced budget cuts, she was assigned to a third. She says that this made it difficult to do her job well. "Ideally, the ratio of students-to-counselor would be 250 or 300 to one. Mine was 1,000 or 1,100 to one. That's too many kids to keep track of. There were a lot of things that we had to skim over or eliminate when we went from two schools to three. I just wasn't able to dig in too deep. When you have too many kids, you end up putting out fires."

Visit Vault at **www.vault.com** for insider company profiles, expert advice, career message boards, expert resume reviews, the Vault Job Board and more.

VAULT CAREER LIBRARY   **119**

During her career, Sullivan had the opportunity to work in a school district where students faced many socioeconomic problems, as well as in a more affluent community. She believes that her role as counselor was equally important in both places. "When I first moved here, I felt like I'd moved to utopia," she says. "I laughed when people complained about some of the little things that were so easily remedied. Kids have so many opportunities here and so much enrichment. But there are kids in need here too. Just because there are fewer socioeconomic problems doesn't mean there's no need. Kids are kids, and kid problems are kid problems no matter where you are. I loved each district for different reasons, and they both were important to me for different reasons."

Changing Careers

CHAPTER 12

After teaching for a number of years, many people decide to leave the classroom in pursuit of other challenges. While some of these people leave education altogether, it is extremely common for people to move into different roles within the education setting. The following pages focus on some of the different possibilities for teachers who want to change careers.

School Administration

Many teachers leave the classroom to pursue a career in school administration. In most cases, to work in school administration you need teaching experience and an advanced degree in school administration.

Higher pay scale

School administrators make significantly higher salaries than classroom teachers, and for many, this is certainly part of the appeal of an administrative role. Like teachers, public school administrators are paid according to a separate pay scale—with different pay being awarded to people at different administrative levels. That is, a district superintendent will earn significantly more than a high school department head.

The exact salaries of administrators varies from district to district, although they usually are paid significantly more than teachers within their districts. So, people who are dedicated to education but want to make more money than classroom teachers may find administration to be a rewarding career change.

But money is not the only reason to pursue a career in school administration. Many teachers move into administrative roles because they enjoy managing people and want to have a say in the way that their school is run, making a difference in the education of a larger group of students. This focus on "system-wide analysis" was what drew James De Francesco into school administration. "It was an opportunity to bring about significant movements not just in my classroom but for the 1,000 kids in the building. As an administrator, you determine where the curriculum goes by determining where you put the money and you determine which children need the extra help. I find the resources to meet my goals for the school; and this position has a far-reaching effect," he says.

Different types of administrative positions

At the high school level, many teachers transition into administrative roles as academic department heads (or assistant department heads). These positions involve overseeing the curriculum initiatives of their department, allocating financial resources throughout their department, organizing any events and activities associated with their departments, and helping teachers to maximize their potential. This requires significant expertise in the academic content area, as well as the ability to manage other adults. In most schools, department heads spend some time in the classroom, but teach fewer classes than the other teachers on staff.

Deans and assistant principals

At the middle school and elementary school levels, teachers often enter school administration as deans or assistant principals. (In small schools they may begin their administrative careers as principals.) Deans are responsible for handling disciplinary problems: when students misbehave in class they are sent to the dean's office, where the dean will then determine the appropriate course of action. Assistant principals oversee a portion of the school—usually either a grade level (or levels), or group of academic subjects. So, a middle school assistant principal might oversee the eighth grade, or the math and science departments in grades six through eight. The primary function of an assistant principal is to oversee budgeting and instructional initiatives and to supervise the teachers. Their focus is not supposed to be on student discipline, although in some schools they do spend a significant amount of time on this issue.

Principals

The principal oversees the deans and the assistant principals and manages the entire school. This may mean being closely involved with hiring decisions, supervising teachers, and working with students. In a very large school, the principal may have limited interactions with teachers and students, concentrating instead on decisions relating to budgets, curriculum, and other large-scale issues.

Other considerations

School principals and assistant principals are public figures in the school community, and they are thus expected to show their support for students by attending school functions that take place in the evening. These may include honors assemblies, athletic events, school plays and other tournaments and competitions that the students participate in.

Principals usually work during the summer months when students and teachers are on vacation. They may have a shortened summer vacation of several weeks, but in general they are expected to use the quiet summer months as a time to prepare the school's budget, oversee building maintenance, create academic plans and otherwise prepare for the upcoming school year.

School districts also have central administration offices, where experienced administrators work to implement changes that will affect the entire district. In addition to superintendents and assistant superintendents, these may include human resources directors, curriculum directors, health education directors, technology directors and others with expertise in a particular subject area. To obtain a job directing a program within an entire school district, it is usually necessary to possess significant administrative experience, either as a principal or assistant principal. In many districts, high-level administrators are also required to have a PhD in an education-related field.

Qualities of a school administrator

To be successful working with teachers, administrators must possess the ability to be tough when they need to be, while at the same time facilitating a team-like environment in the school community. "Administrators should see the curriculum as a collaborative effort, something they will work on with teachers," De Francesco says. "As an assistant principal or principal you should give teachers a voice. This is something you also need to do with the students; you give students what they need to be successful. Equality doesn't always mean giving everyone the same thing in education. I give the extra level of support that shows I understand that you have a lot to do as a teacher already."

Administrators also need the ability to think quickly on their feet, and to make important decisions on a moment's notice. Because they work closely with many people—including students, teachers and parents—they often have to handle difficult decisions quickly. To do this effectively, they need confidence in their own decision-making abilities as well as sophisticated communication skills.

Preparing for a career in school administration

Teachers with an interest in becoming administrators should consider working towards a master's degree in school administration. Regardless of whether or not teachers choose to go into administration, this master's

Visit Vault at **www.vault.com** for insider company profiles, expert advice, career message boards, expert resume reviews, the Vault Job Board and more.

VAULT CAREER LIBRARY   **123**

degree will enable them to move higher on the teacher pay scale, and is therefore a worthwhile investment. In fact, many teachers who obtain master's degrees in administration never actually apply for administrative positions.

In large districts with administrative shortages, subsidized master's degrees are sometimes available for teachers who are identified as having great potential to succeed in an administrative capacity. After completing their subsidized degrees, these educators are usually required to work as administrators in their districts for two or more years.

Transitional opportunities

To become noticed as a school leader, a teacher might move from the classroom into a staff development (or teacher mentoring) position. This is an opportunity for teachers to demonstrate their ability to work with adults, to oversee large-scale school initiatives, and to work more closely with the existing administrative staff.

Teachers can also demonstrate their interest in school administration by volunteering to serve on school budgeting committees, hiring committees, or on curriculum-planning teams. All of these can help someone with administrative potential to be recognized as a staff member who is capable of handling large-scale projects and making good decisions. This is also a good opportunity for teachers to get an inside peek at the realities of school administration, and to decide if this is a career path they want to follow.

De Francesco believes that most schools offer plenty of opportunities for enthusiastic teachers to gain practical, administrative experience. He says that many school principals are "looking for teachers who are willing to take the ball and run with it. Even if you just sign up to be a trip coordinator, or an advisor, you need these interim steps to becoming an administrator."

A Day in the Life: Middle School Assistant Principal

After the events of September 11, 2001 James De Francesco began to think about changing careers, and trying to do something that would make a positive difference in the world. He was already a successful professional, having begun his career working for New York City Mayor Ed Koch as a manager of contract compliance—a job that included negotiating with the New York City teachers' union. Eventually he moved into real estate, where he worked for many years on large-scale New York City construction projects.

In the fall of 2002 De Francesco began the New York City Teaching Fellows program, participating in their Math Immersion program, which gives new teachers a crash course in mathematics in addition to the teacher training that is a standard part of the Teaching Fellows program.

A tough start

De Francesco began his teaching career at one of the roughest middle schools in the city. Although this was challenging, he says that he never worried about his own safety. "The safety issues in the school were predominantly student-on-student concerns. Random, wanton violence directed at teachers was unheard of. However, in a school like this you do have to be concerned about your state of mind. It can be depressing, nerve-wracking, and tense. In that sense it's going to be a debilitating atmosphere for a teacher. You can have the greatest lesson plan in world and one kid comes into your classroom and does something stupid. This sets everyone else off and completely ruins your lesson."

The challenges of math

While teachers of other subjects often say that paper grading is one of their biggest challenges, De Francesco says that for a math teacher the biggest challenge is making the material accessible to students, something that is particularly difficult in a school where most students are behind grade level.

De Francesco describes one math lesson that he found to be extremely successful. "I went to supermarket and bought the most colorful boxes I could find and we used those for models when I taught the lesson on surface area. The students' assignment was to find their own box at home and bring it in. Then the next day the students found the surface areas of their own boxes. This made the subject personal, and it forced the students to engage their families. They told their parents 'I need a box for this lesson we're doing in Mr. D's class.' And this conversation gets translated to the classroom. The next day the students were saying, 'Oh, you buy this brand, my family buys another brand,' and 'Oh, you shop at Western Beef—a supermarket in the area—I shop at that store too.' This all made the lesson extremely accessible and real-world to them."

In addition to making lessons accessible, James believes that math teachers need real expertise in their subject area. "Do you need to be able to teach

Visit Vault at **www.vault.com** for insider company profiles, expert advice, career message boards, expert resume reviews, the Vault Job Board and more.

VAULT CAREER LIBRARY   125

calculus in order too teach third grade math? No. Do you need to be able to understand it to teach third grade math? Yes. You need to know where the students are coming from and going to—you need to understand how it fits into the arc of the curriculum."

Transitioning to administration

Eventually, De Francesco transferred from his school in Brooklyn to one that was much closer to his home. Soon afterwards, he became a math coach, mentoring the other math teachers at his school. This gave him the opportunity to attend math teacher conferences in New York City, and at one of these workshops he was approached by the conference facilitator about a program offered through the Bank Street School designed to train talented teachers to become school administrators. When this opportunity arose, he realized that an administrative position was the perfect way to combine his experience as a teacher and as an executive to affect the educational environment of an entire school.

In his role as an assistant principal, James sees himself as someone who is there to help his teachers succeed. He says that administrators should see themselves as "a resource to teachers. If that means making copies of a test for all the teachers, then that's what you do to build confidence and respect. The best bosses give you what you need, and then step out of the way. Teachers don't need someone hovering. If you can give someone the things that you know he needs, that person will come back to you and ask for assistance when he needs it. He'll come back because he knows you were there for him," he says.

Advice for new teachers

De Francesco's advice to new teachers is that they put all the energy they can into motivating their students. "If you really are interested in teaching, you need to show your students that you are interested in teaching. Show your students that you are passionate. If you go into a classroom and show the kids that you're pumped, you have them already. If you're like the teacher from "Ferris Bueller's Day Off" who says, 'anyone…anyone?' you're dead. I don't say this glibly, because I understand that this is not an easy profession to do well, and to do correctly. But you have to do it that way because you are dealing with children. They'd rather be sleeping, or out on the handball court—they don't care about reading *Julius Caesar* or learning the Pythagorean theorem. You have to make them care about it. You can't do it every period, but you have to try every period."

A day in De Francesco's life

4:50 a.m.:	Wake up.
6:30 a.m.:	Drop daughter off at train station.
6:50 a.m.:	Arrive at school. Morning meeting with principal and dean—recap the previous day and discuss what we will do today. Check and see which staff members will not be at work today, and which subs will be in the building. Go over the paperwork that needs to be done, and who will do it. Meet with any parents who need to come in early for conferences.
7:25 a.m.:	Open doors for the students who have breakfast at school. If the weather is bad, supervise the students who are waiting in the auditorium for the bell to ring.
7:45 a.m.:	Escort students into the building, to their first period classes. Visit all 13 classes in my academy. Speak to the kids, greet each of them and make sure they're fine—that no one has a black eye or cuts on their face—and wish them all a good day.
8:00 a.m.:	Meet with parents. Check in-house suspension room and make sure that the students who are supposed to be there are there. Check on the students who came late, and who are doing assignments in the auditorium. Talk to the students who are chronically late.
8:30 a.m.:	Second period begins. Facilitate a meeting with several math teachers. Go over curriculum pacing calendars, testing cycles and portfolios. Share ideas for lessons and give teachers the opportunity to share their stories from the trenches.
9:20 a.m.:	Stand in the hallway to supervise the changing of classes. Start paperwork. Take calls from parents. Visit a class where the kids are acting up.
10:10 a.m.:	Go to the cafeteria for first lunch period. Arrive before the students to set a tone. Go outside with the students if it's a nice day.

Visit Vault at **www.vault.com** for insider company profiles, expert advice, career message boards, expert resume reviews, the Vault Job Board and more.

VAULT CAREER LIBRARY   **127**

10:54 a.m.:	Go upstairs and visit all 13 classes in my academy again. Make sure no one cut school during lunch. Talk with students, make some jokes. Take calls from parents. If a student is acting up, assist the teacher with discipline.
11:42 a.m.:	Take calls from parents. If there are discipline problems, visit any classrooms where the students are acting up.
12:30 p.m.:	Now that the last lunch period is over, deal with the aftermath of lunch. If there was a fight, try to get the kids calmed down. Check e-mail, talk to parents and work on math curriculum maps and end-of-year award ceremony programs.
1:20 p.m.:	Get into dismissal mode. Make sure that the buses are showing up, and that school security is making sure that high school kids aren't hanging around the school. Finally, make sure that the staircases are free and clear.
2:02 p.m.:	First dismissal. Get ready for after-school programs and tutoring. Make sure the gymnasium is ready for the community organization that rents it in the afternoons.
2:20 p.m.:	Circulate the building. Make sure all kids are where they should be.
2:30 p.m.:	Second dismissal. Circulate the building again.
3:00 p.m.:	Afternoon cabinet meeting. Examine the things that happened today. Discuss the budget and the progress of the students. This is our opportunity to focus on these things without interruption.
5:30 p.m.:	Leave the building.

In the evening: Spend between one and four hours working on curriculum plans and paperwork.

Staff Development Positions

In recent years, school districts have placed an increasing emphasis on staff development, and encouraging teachers to see themselves as lifelong learners. In addition to requirements for teachers to earn graduate credits or otherwise continue their education, many schools also have staff development programs that are designed to help teachers improve their skills on an ongoing basis. The facilitators of these programs are usually referred to as "staff developers." In the role of mentor teachers, staff developers will often provide new teachers with guidance and support, visiting classrooms and helping teachers improve their skills. They also lead staff meetings that focus on useful new pedagogical techniques. Staff developers are seasoned classroom teachers who are selected for this role because of proven success in the classroom.

Many schools have designated staff development periods during the school week. These may take place during the school day, or after the students have left the building. They may involve the entire staff or be designated for one department (i.e., all the math teachers).

Education and implementation

In addition to educating teachers about general pedagogical techniques, staff developers assist teachers when district-wide changes are implemented. So, if a school system decides to adopt a citywide curriculum that is vastly different from what teachers have used in the past, the staff developer will help teachers understand what is expected of them, and how they can adapt the new curriculum to their own teaching styles. Because teachers are frequently skeptical of big, district-wide changes, the staff developer helps reassure them that the new procedures can be useful, and the transition will be a painless one.

The responsibility for mentoring new teachers is a very important part of a staff developer's role. This involves talking with new teachers about their struggles, helping them plan effective lessons and visiting their classrooms. Many people leave the teaching profession after a short time, and a skilled staff developer can play an important role in encouraging people to stick with the profession.

Conducting staff meetings can be a challenge for the staff developer. The busy teachers who attend these sessions are frequently tired or overwhelmed by their workload—and the staff developer is responsible for maintaining their interest and attention. Therefore, it is critical that a staff developer makes sure that staff training sessions cover useful and practical information. Most teachers are eager to gain new skills and learn new techniques, but at the same time they will quickly grow impatient with meetings that they feel are a waste of time.

Notes from the field

Steve Tullin, a New York City staff developer, says that as a staff developer, "You have to present information that's useful, engaging and interesting; a lot of it is a matter of presenting. I had people who came to the table with papers to mark, and I had to fight that issue. It's not the easiest thing to do and requires skills, a lot of thinking on your feet and a lot of preparation." In fact, Tullin says that when he began his role as a staff developer, he and the other developer in his building would rehearse their training sessions before presenting them to the staff.

While staff developers are chosen for this role based on their skills in the classroom, they often find that working with adults poses new challenges. Success as a staff developer requires strong people skills and a sincere desire to help teachers succeed. This genuine desire to help is critical, as a staff developer who simply wants to be seen as an expert is unlikely to be popular among the staff. Tullin says that staff developers should "formulate a community so the teachers don't rebel and aren't resentful. You need to have a good sense of humor. You need to have courtesy and respect for teachers, just like in the classroom. You need a rapport with the people you're presenting to."

Diplomacy needed, security wanted

Staff developers are usually paid according to the regular teacher pay scale. But while they are teachers according to the pay scale, they usually work more closely with the school administration than regular teachers. A well-respected staff developer may even become involved in administrative activities such as budgeting. The downside of this is that staff developers sometimes feel caught between the teachers and administrators, because in a way they are both. "As a staff developer you're walking a tightrope with respect to the administration because you're working with principals and assistant principals, but you're also a teacher. By rights I shouldn't have been reporting on the teacher attendance to staff development periods, but I was forced into that role," Tullin says.

Another downside to working as a staff developer is that when a district is forced to make budget cuts, staff development positions are often eliminated. While most staff developers have enough seniority to be guaranteed a job, they may be placed back in the classroom when this occurs—something that can be a rough adjustment for someone who has spent years working with adult staff members. This uncertainty as to the stability of their role within the school is a source of stress for many staff developers. On the flip side, there is a demand for experienced teacher trainers in many areas. Tullin, for example, is officially retired from the New York City public schools but continues to work in the public schools three days a week as a private contractor, leading staff development sessions in two different high schools.

Other Careers for Trained Educators

Teachers who want to work outside the school environment may be able to find education-related corporate jobs. These positions frequently have higher salaries than teaching positions, and may also offer more opportunities for advancement. The following are a few examples of areas within the corporate sector where a background in education is valued.

Corporate trainer

Large companies often have elaborate employee training programs that may cover topics such as company benefits, anti-discrimination/sexual harassment policies and specific job-related skills. Many corporations see their training programs as an important way to develop a skilled workforce and will eagerly hire a trained teacher to fulfill this role. However, in order to obtain a position that involves instructing people on highly technical subjects, a teacher may need to possess prior knowledge of these topics.

Educational publishing

Many textbook companies need trained educators to help create educational products. Writers and editors of educational content must be familiar with the typical curricula for different grade levels, and with the educational standards imposed by different states upon their schools. Most importantly, educational writers need to be able to organize information in a way that allows for easy use in the classroom environment. All educational materials must be written at an age-appropriate level, and presented in a way that is easy for children to understand.

In addition to producing books for students, most K-12 textbook companies produce "teacher's editions" that include strategies for teaching the material covered in the student textbooks. This requires extensive knowledge of different teaching methods and strategies.

In addition to creating traditional textbooks, there are several large companies that publish test preparation materials for K-12 standardized tests. The creation of these materials relies on the talents of educators who understand the standardized testing process, and different strategies for developing students' test-taking skills.

Educational software development

At one time, educational software was primarily purchased by parents and used by children at home. Now, however, the growing presence of computers in schools across the country has made computer-based instruction a significant area within the field of education. While the technical aspects of creating software don't necessarily call for the skills of a trained teacher, the content of the information presented on the software does call for personnel with a background in education. In addition to presenting lessons in a clearly understood, age-appropriate manner, lessons presented through software programs must be designed so that a teacher can facilitate their use while working with large groups of students (unless the program is designed for independent student learning).

Educational software companies also frequently hire educators to travel to different classrooms to assist teachers with implementing their products. This type of position may involve extensive traveling, although in large cities travel may be limited to the metropolitan region.

Distance education

With the advent of online courses, home study programs are now more popular than ever before. While distance education programs are usually designed for adult learners, many schools that offer distance learning will welcome the skills of a trained educator regardless of what grade level the teacher has previously taught. The educator's role within the sphere of distance education may involve creating course content and developing the methods by which it will be delivered to students.

Lifestyle

CHAPTER 13

Teachers have a lifestyle that is both more stressful and more flexible than that of people working in other fields. The following pages outline the most important aspects you need to know about the teaching lifestyle.

Women and Minorities

Education is an inclusive field, and for many years, education was one of the few fields where educated women could pursue careers. Not only could women find work as teachers, but they were also able to rise to administrative positions during times when women were severely limited in other professions. It's fair to say that while the "glass ceiling" continues to be a reality for women in fields like investment banking, it is much less of a reality in the field of education.

Modern attitudes towards gender have also changed the role of men in education, with more men becoming elementary school educators now than in the past. And rather than placing a stigma on male elementary teachers, schools now actively seek out male candidates, because current educational theory supports the idea that it is beneficial for children to have male and female role models.

Education is also a profession with a history of providing people of color with professional opportunities. However, in the past these opportunities were often confined to schools that served minority communities. Even after segregation was abolished, it was difficult for teachers of color to find work in predominately white school districts. Fortunately, this has changed, and it is now possible for minority teachers to find employment and success in any school, regardless of the demographic makeup of the student body.

Common Misconceptions

There is a common misconception that teachers have relaxing jobs. People outside the field often believe that with short days and summers off, teachers make good salaries while working less than people in other professions. The truth is that a career in education is an incredibly demanding field with a high level of burn out. Yes, teachers do end their official days around 3:00 p.m., but they typically start earlier in the day than other professionals. Furthermore, most teachers spend a significant percentage of the "free time" on work-related activities, with many of them struggling to find a balance between work and their personal lives. The responsibility for paper grading, lesson planning, making phone calls to parents and other tasks is limitless, and most teachers need to make a conscious effort to find time for themselves. After a number of years in the classroom, many teachers find that they are better able to juggle the teaching workload, but even after years in the classroom, it is a profession that demands a great deal of energy and that can cause a great deal of stress.

Furthermore, a career working with children is not one that you can easily walk away from at the end of the day. Most teachers worry about the split-second decisions they make in the classroom and about the impact that these decisions may have on children's lives. And when a child is going through difficult times, they will hurt along with the child. As many of the professionals interviewed in this book have stated, a good teacher must maintain a healthy perspective and find time to pursue interests and relationships outside of the school environment; very few completely succeed at forgetting about their students the minute they walk out of the school doors.

An endless vacation?

No one should enter the field of education simply for the time off. The job is too demanding, and a few weeks of summer vacation will not be a worthwhile tradeoff for someone who enters the field looking for time off. However, for those people who sincerely enjoy education, the vacation time is certainly a benefit of the profession. Many teachers use their vacation time to travel or pursue hobbies and avocations that they don't have time for during the school year. People with children of their own also find it convenient to be on the same schedule as their children. Once their children enter school, they are usually at home when their children are home, which may enable them to save money on childcare and to spend extended periods of time with their children during the holidays.

The lifestyle of a teacher is both challenging and rewarding. People who work in education are some of the most hard-working professionals in the workforce—education is not the right field for someone who is simply looking for a way to pay the bills. At the same time, those who love the field of education find it hard to imagine doing anything else. If you have a sincere passion for teaching and love of children, then you can be happy in this profession.

Teacher Salaries

A recent report from the American Federation of Teachers states that the average salary of an American schoolteacher is $47,602. However, it is difficult to assess the meaning of this average because of the great disparity in teacher salaries throughout the country. The following section will give you examples of teacher salaries in different types of school districts, and an understanding of how teacher pay scales work.

Sample teacher salary: Detroit

Virtually all public school teachers, and many private school teachers, are paid according to a scale that awards salary increases as teachers gain classroom experience and advanced degrees. The example below is an excerpt from the pay scale that is currently used in the Detroit public schools:

Experience	Bachelor's degree	Master's degree
Beginning salary:	$38,680	$40,523
5 years:	$45,764	$51,523
10 years:	$60,811	$70,747

Teachers in public schools typically make much more money than teachers in private schools. Below are the starting salaries and maximum salaries for teachers in New York City public schools, as compared to the teachers represented by the Federation of Catholic Teachers (a union that represents teachers in 200 New York City Catholic schools).

Visit Vault at **www.vault.com** for insider company profiles, expert advice, career message boards, expert resume reviews, the Vault Job Board and more.

V/\ULT CAREER LIBRARY   **135**

Sample teacher salary: New York City

New York City teachers in public and Catholic schools:

	Public schools	**Catholic schools**
Beginning salary:	$45,530	$29,893
Maximum salary:	$74,796	$41,745

Teacher salaries also vary widely based on geographical region, with teachers in urban and suburban areas typically making more money than teachers in rural areas. In many cases, the salaries of teachers in rural areas are comparable to those in private city schools. The following are excerpts from a rural area in West Virginia, where teacher pay is notoriously low:

Sample teacher salary: Rural West Virginia

Minimum and maximum salaries, Doddridge County, West Virginia:

	Bachelor's	**Master's**
Beginning salary:	$28,270	$30,997
Maximum salary:	$30,997	$39,884

As the above examples illustrate, teacher salaries are inconsistent throughout the United States. As a result, some teachers decide where to work and live based upon the pay that teachers earn in a given school district. Of course, for some people, salary is not the most important factor when applying for jobs, but the reality is that for most people it is one factor.

In most cases, all professionals in a school setting (with the exception of administrators) are paid according to the same pay schedule. This includes counselors, media specialists, physical education, art and music teachers.

Many education reformers believe that the inequality in teacher salaries contributes to the inequality in American schools. While urban school districts often pay teachers reasonably well, wealthy suburban communities usually pay them better. And because many urban schools are notoriously difficult places to teach, teachers have little incentive to teach in these schools when they will get paid more somewhere else.

Supplementary Sources of Income

While most teachers cannot earn a higher salary than the maximum stipulated by their local district, there are a number of ways for motivated teachers to increase their annual earnings. Many of these opportunities are located within the school setting. So, although these extra jobs can be demanding, they give teachers an opportunity to become more integrated into the school community, and do not require teachers to spend time commuting to a second job.

Teaching summer school

Virtually every school district has summer school programs. These are often remedial academic programs, but may also include sports camps, theater camps, art classes, driver's education, and other enrichment programs. The summer school schedule is usually less intense than that of the regular school year. For example, many school systems have shorter school days, or a four-day-per-week schedule, during the summer months.

In many districts, students from several different schools may be sent to one location for summer school. This means that teachers who work summer school may be required to work in a different school building from the one where they normally teach.

Most districts pay their teachers on a biweekly basis year-round (meaning that teachers continue to receive their paychecks during the summer months). Therefore, those teachers who work summer school are able to earn a large sum of money on top of their regular salaries.

After-school tutoring programs

The No Child Left Behind Act mandates that students in under-performing schools be given the opportunity to attend supplementary after-school programs. These government-funded programs are operated by private corporations rather than by the school district. However, they heavily recruit teachers in the host schools to work in these programs.

Visit Vault at **www.vault.com** for insider company profiles, expert advice, career message boards, expert resume reviews, the Vault Job Board and more.

VAULT CAREER LIBRARY   137

These tutoring programs often utilize heavily scripted curricula, which means that teachers who work in these programs do not need to spend much time planning. In these situations, teachers are assigned to small groups of students, which also makes this type of teaching less stressful than the regular school day. In addition to after-school programs, some schools have Saturday school programs, giving teachers an additional opportunity to supplement their incomes.

Private tutoring

Many teachers do private tutoring, one-on-one, with students in their homes. This gives teachers a great deal of flexibility and the opportunity to set their own hourly pay rates. Some teachers fall into this role after being approached by a parent or colleague. Others sign up with a private tutoring company that matches them up with families who are looking for a tutor. Still others may promote their tutoring services online.

Most teachers will not do private tutoring (for pay) with a student whom they currently have in class. This is generally considered unethical, not to mention that it is an invitation for the teacher to be accused of favoritism by students, parents and administrators. It is usually considered acceptable, however, for a teacher to do private tutoring with a former student or a student who attends the school where the teacher works.

Extracurricular activities

Teachers who agree to lead a sports team, academic club, music or theater group are compensated for their time. Although the income teachers earn through these endeavors can be sizeable, they are often paid in a lump sum that is not really commensurate with the number of hours it takes to lead the practices and attend the events associated with a given extracurricular activity. For example, a high school football coach not only has to lead practices on a daily basis but also has to attend football games that may take place in locations throughout the state. So it's important for teachers to remember that while extracurricular activities can be incredibly rewarding, they are very time-consuming, and the time spent may not be accurately reflected in their financial compensation.

Benefits Packages

While teacher salaries are not always adequate, most public schools have generous benefits packages that offset these salaries. Most public school teachers have both health and dental insurance. They are also frequently enrolled in pension plans that accrue in value throughout their years of service within a district. Additionally, many schools offer 403(b) plans that allow teachers to contribute to a retirement fund from their pre-tax dollars. (A 403(b) plan works the same way as the more common 401(k) plan. The difference is simply that 403(b) plans are only for government employees.)

Private schools are also often generous in teacher benefits packages. However, private schools are not required to offer their employees any particular benefits, and the packages they offer can vary dramatically. Therefore, before accepting a position in a private school it is wise for a teacher to ask for a breakdown of the benefits that will be provided.

Merit-Based Raises

In an effort to reform the education system, many politicians currently advocate merit-based raises rather than overall salary increases to teacher pay schedules. The theory behind this is that to attract the best and brightest people into the field of education, teachers should be rewarded for excellent performance rather than years in the classroom. If implemented, merit-based raises would pay teachers according to a system more similar to that in corporate America.

A controversial issue

Many in the education community oppose merit-based raises. They argue that it is difficult to assess a teacher's performance in a comprehensive way. Student performance on multiple-choice tests is often the basis by which merit-based raises are awarded, and most teachers believe that there is already too much emphasis on standardized testing. Thus, they fear that a salary schedule based on how well students do on multiple-choice would only result in more "teaching to the test."

Another criticism of merit-based raises is that this type of program might dissuade teachers from teaching in the highest needs schools, which have a history of low test scores. As a way of addressing this criticism, many districts with merit-based raises also offer financial bonuses or student loan forgiveness to teachers who work in high-needs schools.

There are also merit-based raise systems that rely more on other factors (such as supervisor evaluations) than on standardized tests. This more comprehensive approach to granting merit-based raises is more palatable to most educators than the standardized testing model.

While still controversial, there are some American school districts that have implemented a merit-based raise system that is acceptable to both the teachers and the community at large.

FINAL
ANALYSIS

Final Analysis

Answering the Call

Many teachers believe that education is their calling. These people often say that they always knew they wanted to be teachers, and they usually follow a traditional path to teacher certification, finding their first teaching jobs immediately after college graduation. If, like them, you know at an early age that education is the right field for you, this can be a fantastic way to enter the profession.

At the same time, many people decide to become educators later in life; just because they've chosen teaching as a second, third or fourth career does not mean that they are any less passionate or successful than the people for whom education is a lifelong calling. There is no one "correct" pathway into the profession. What is necessary in an aspiring teacher; however, is a belief in the unlimited potential of students and a dedication to providing them with the best learning experiences possible.

Ups and Downs

The challenges of a teaching career are many. Teachers juggle intense workloads. They often struggle to communicate with students and parents in an effective way. They sometimes feel isolated in the classroom because of their limited contact with other adults. And teachers' salaries, while living wages, are smaller than those of many other professionals. Thus, a career in education is not the easiest path to follow, and it's possible to come up with a host of reasons why someone might choose an alternate career.

However, many people do choose to become classroom teachers, school counselors, administrators and other education professionals. And a large percentage of these people say there is nothing else they would rather do. The satisfaction of working with students—whether children or adults—can be unparalleled. Teachers truly have a unique opportunity to watch their students grow, and to make a difference in people's lives.

Making the Commitment

Those who enter the classroom should do so with the understanding that the first few years will be difficult—and they should also understand that things will get easier with experience. Many of those who leave the field of education do so before giving themselves enough time to hone their skills and learn effective ways of managing their workloads.

Those teachers who are most successful in the classroom see themselves as lifelong learners who believe in their abilities to become better teachers. They are continually striving to learn new techniques that will help their students absorb information.

A career in education is not right for everyone, but it can be a wonderful profession for someone who is prepared for the challenges it offers. If you believe that education is the right field for you, there is a great demand for teachers in the United States, and countless students out there who are eager to learn and ready to benefit from your talents.

APPENDIX

EDUCATION
CAREERS

Resources

The following resources contain useful information for new teachers and people considering a career in education. In addition to the information included here, local school district websites usually contain extensive information about teaching requirements, applying for jobs and specific schools. The websites of universities that offer degrees in education can also be important sources of information for new teachers.

Organizations

National Center for Education Statistics: nces.ed.gov

A government-sponsored site that collects data relating to all aspects of education.

National Association for Education of Young Children (NAEYC): nayeyc.org

Professional organization focusing on the education of children from preschool through age eight.

National Middle School Association: nmsa.org

School Social Work Association of America (SSWAA): sswaa.org

Association for Supervision and Curriculum Development: ascd.org

A professional organization that helps teachers and administrators plan meaningful curricula for children at all grade levels.

American School Counselor Association: schoolcounselor.org

Progressive Education Network (PEN): progressiveed.org

A source of information for anyone interested in progressive education. Their website contains job postings for teaching positions in addition to general information about progressive schools.

Alternative Certification Programs

Teach for America: teachforamerica.org

New York City Teaching Fellows: NYCTeachingFellows.org

National Center for Alternative Certification: Teach-Now.org

An organization that provides comprehensive information about alternative teacher certification programs throughout the United States.

The New Teacher Project: tntp.org

A nonprofit organization that manages alternative certification programs in over 200 school districts.

New Leaders for New Schools

A program that selects top teachers and trains them to become school administrators in hard-to-staff urban districts.

Teachers' Unions

National Education Association (NEA): nea.org

The largest teacher's union in the United States, representing teachers in thousands of communities throughout the United States.

American Federation of Teachers (AFT-CIO): aft.org

The second-largest teacher's union in the United States.

United Federation of Teachers (UFT): uft.org

The union representing public school teachers in New York City.

Websites

greatschools.net

A comprehensive database listing public, private and charter schools throughout the United States, with ratings from members of the community.

publicschoolreview.com

Information about thousands of public schools in locations throughout the United States.

insideschools.org

An independent source of information about public New York City schools.

Recommended Reading

Teachers Have it Easy: The Big Sacrifices and Small Salaries of America's Teachers, Daniel Moulthrop, 2006

A discussion of teacher salaries in the United States. While the book emphasizes a controversial approach to teacher salary reform, it contains a great deal of information that will be useful to people on all sides of the salary reform debate.

Other People's Children: Cultural Conflict in the Classroom, Lisa Delpit, 2006

A discussion of the communication problems that exist between teachers and students in American schools, particularly when the teacher is from a different cultural background than the students.

The Shame of the Nation: Restoration of Apartheid Schooling In America, Jonathan Kozol, 2004

One of the most recent titles from a prominent critic of America's education system. This book offers a sharp criticism of the low expectations of students in low-income communities throughout the United States. This book and others by Kozol will offer many valuable insights for anyone considering a career in urban education.

The Moral Imperative of School Leadership , Michael Fullan, 2003

Discusses the moral obligation of school leaders to create successful learning environments, while focusing on the ways that school leaders can implement changes that will benefit students. Fullan is considered a leader in the school reform movement and all of his books will be of interest to the aspiring teacher.

Visit Vault at **www.vault.com** for insider company profiles, expert advice, career message boards, expert resume reviews, the Vault Job Board and more.

V/\ULT CAREER LIBRARY   **149**

Understanding by Design, Grant P. Wiggins, 2005

An approach to curriculum development that focuses on "backwards design": identifying a learning objective and then creating a lesson plan to meet the objectives.

Shouting Won't Grow Dendrites: Techniques for Managing a Brain-Compatible Classroom, Marsha L. Tate, 2006

Information about brain research and techniques for classroom management that facilitate student achievement and deal with chronic behavior problems.

Conscious Classroom Management: Unlocking the Secrets of Great Teaching, Rick Smith, 2004

Practical information for managing behavior problems in the classroom and facilitating constructive student/teacher relationships.

Differentiated Instruction Strategies: One Size Doesn't Fit All, Gayle H. Gregory, 2006

A practical approach to adapting curriculum to meet the needs of every student.

How the Brain Learns, David A. Sousa, 2006

Research on how the human brain processes information, with suggestions for how educators can use this knowledge to create successful learning environments.

Classroom Strategies for Interactive Learning, Doug Buehl, 2001

Literacy strategies for secondary teachers in all subject areas.

About the Author

Jennifer Baker taught seventh grade English in Brooklyn for four years as a part of the New York City Teaching Fellows Program. She now is a curriculum developer and educational writer.

Visit Vault at **www.vault.com** for insider company profiles, expert advice, career message boards, expert resume reviews, the Vault Job Board and more.

VAULT CAREER LIBRARY   151

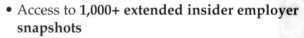
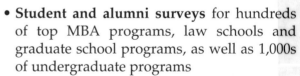